ALL SOCCER FORMATIONS: THE ULTIMATE GUIDE TO POSITIONING

ALL SOCCER FORMATIONS: THE ULTIMATE GUIDE TO POSITIONING

Arthur M. Mutebi

© Arthur M Mutebi 2015

This work is copyright. Apart from any use as permitted under the Copyright Act 1968, no part may be reproduced by any process without prior written permission from the author.

ISBN: 978-0-646-94233-9

arthur.mutebi@gmail.com

Contents

Preface 5
Summary 6
How to interpret this book 6
LEVEL 1 9
LEVEL 2 11
LEVEL 3 17
LEVEL 4 38
LEVEL 5 83
LEVEL 6 150
LEVEL 7 217
LEVEL 8 262
LEVEL 9 283
LEVEL 10 289
Formation Index 292

Preface

This book was bred purely from inspiration and love for life, and for the game. It is through life's moments that the game lives and only such a place can secrets like these be revealed. It is my hope that this book can change the nature of how soccer is enjoyed and that it can inspire others to aspire for love in life.

Summary

What's in this book?

This book contains the first known complete classification, illustration and descriptive analysis of *all the 512* possible 10 man soccer formations.

Why use this book?

This book provides football and mathematics with the first categorical description of all soccer formations, their names and how to describe them. This catapults its prime use being the ability for analytics to examine formations on and off the pitch allowing more information in understanding football solutions. Mathematically, this book is the first to describe and illustrate all possible ways of attaining the number 10 by whole integers and geometrically, uses of which are yet to be explored.

How to use this book

This book must be used with careful analysis of both the external elements of the game and internal contents of the book, in relation to the reader's use of it. It was developed with *aim to guide* and as such readers must use it to develop better understanding of football problems and probable solutions as opposed to attaining winning strategies. It's the analytics' responsibility to understand requirements of the game in relation to player ability, opposition tactics and team mental culture. Used correctly, this book will be a useful tool to anyone with the need to understand better and/or to control the beautiful game!

How to interpret this book

Please note:

a)　The keeper, the vital role which completes all formations, is to be kept in thought when analysing and/or using these formations.

b) Neutral players are roaming players (i.e. neither completely attacking nor defensive) and so are neutral formations.

c) All non-neutral formations are mirror formations (e.g 1-2-3-4 is mirrored but different from 4-3-2-1)

The analysis provided in this book is descriptive and based on 8 simple tools/metrics. These metrics analyse the shape, spread and positioning of players in each formation.

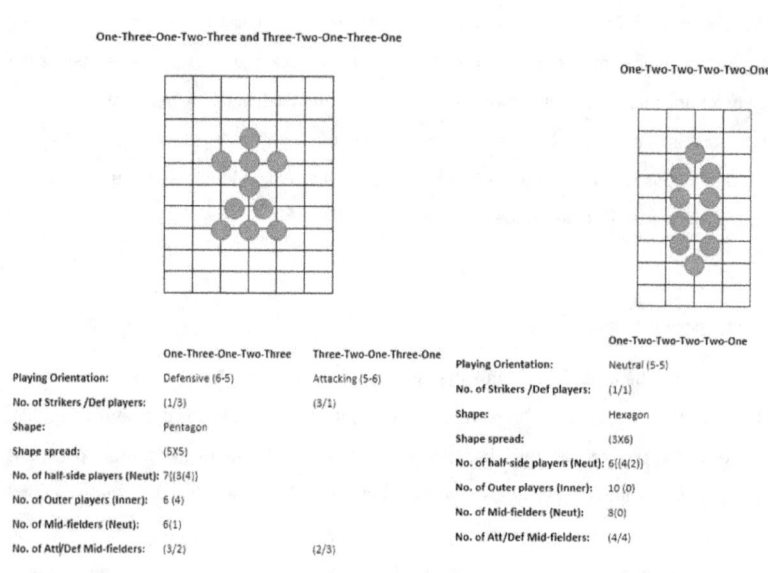

	One-Three-One-Two-Three	Three-Two-One-Three-One
Playing Orientation:	Defensive (6-5)	Attacking (5-6)
No. of Strikers /Def players:	(1/3)	(3/1)
Shape:	Pentagon	
Shape spread:	(5X5)	
No. of half-side players (Neut):	7{(3(4)}	
No. of Outer players (Inner):	6 (4)	
No. of Mid-fielders (Neut):	6(1)	
No. of Att/Def Mid-fielders:	(3/2)	(2/3)

	One-Two-Two-Two-Two-One
Playing Orientation:	Neutral (5-5)
No. of Strikers /Def players:	(1/1)
Shape:	Hexagon
Shape spread:	(3X6)
No. of half-side players (Neut):	6{(4(2)}
No. of Outer players (Inner):	10 (0)
No. of Mid-fielders (Neut):	8(0)
No. of Att/Def Mid-fielders:	(4/4)

The metrics used and their meanings are:

1. **Playing Orientation:** .e.g *Defensive (6-5);* This refers to whether the formation is attacking, neutral, or defensive and the concurrent number of players available for these roles. It is determined by the equating line along the width of the formation. Neutral players are classified as both attacking and defensive.

2. **No. of Strikers /Def players:** This metric refers to the number of outer strikers and defenders i.e. borderline players; it's useful for understanding both the defensive and attacking blueprints of the formation.

3. **Shape:** This is an important metric, it refers to the geometric form taken on by the outer most players (i.e. triangle, rectangle, trapezium etc.). It's useful for understanding the spread of the formation and number of outer and inner players.

4. **Shape spread:** This metric describes the levels expressed by each formation; it describes the distribution and spread of the players. E.g. Formation x with (5X5) is five levels of players across (width-wise) and five down (length-wise).

5. **No. of half-side players (Neutral):** This metric refers to the number of players available on one half of the formation. It's useful to understand the number of players available against wing play and how the formation spreads. E.g. Metric 7{(3(4)} directly translates to a total of 7 wide players, with 3 completely wide and 4 neutral (roaming).

6. **No. of Outer players (Inner):** This metric is derived from understanding the geometric form (i.e. whether the formation is triangle, rectangle, trapezium, etc...). This metric is very useful as it determines the *preferred* outer players for all formations and concurrently midfield positions, *on a rectangle based pitch*.

7. **No. of Mid-fielders (Neutral):** This metric is based on the determined geometric form; it refers to the number of middle players excluding the borderline attackers and defenders. Neutral players in odd level formations (e.g. level 3, level 5 etc.) are shown in brackets.

8. **No. of Att/Def Mid-fielders:** This metric refers to the number of complete attacking/defensive mid-fielders available. This metric may be changed to suit the users liking.

LEVEL 1

Formations: 1
Symmetrically neutral: 1

One-One-One-One-One-One-One-One-One-One (A)

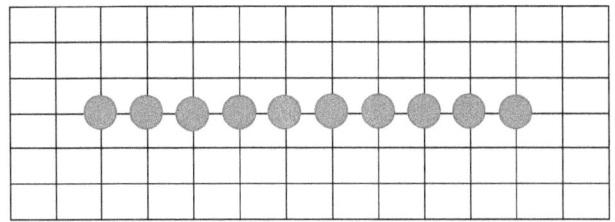

One-One-One-One-One-One-One-One-One-One (A)

Playing Orientation:	Neutral (10-10)
No. of Strikers /Def players:	(10/10)
Shape:	Linear
Shape spread:	(10X1)
No. of half-side players (Neut):	5{(5(0)}
No. of Outer players (Inner):	10 (0)
No. of Mid-fielders (Neut):	0(0)
No. of Att/Def Mid-fielders:	(0/0)

LEVEL 2

Formations: 9

Symmetrically neutral: 1

One-Nine and Nine-One

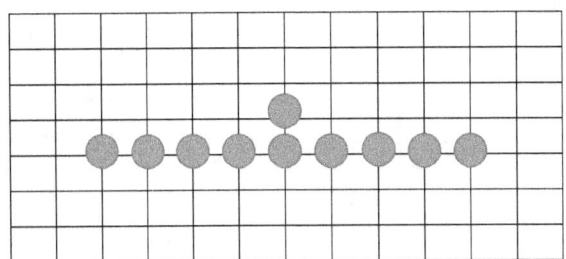

	One-Nine	Nine-One
Playing Orientation:	Defensive (9-1)	Attacking (1-9)
No. of Strikers/Def players:	(1/9)	(9/1)
Shape:	Triangle	
Shape spread:	(9X2)	
No. of half-side players (Neut):	6{(4(2)}	
No. of Outer players (Inner):	10 (0)	
No. of Mid-fielders (Neut):	0(0)	
No. of Att/Def Mid-fielders:	(0/0)	(0/0)

Two-Eight and Eight-Two

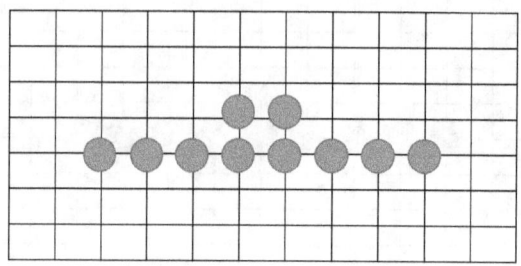

	Two-Eight	Eight-Two
Playing Orientation:	Defensive (8-2)	Attacking (2-8)
No. of Strikers/Def players:	(2/8)	(8/2)
Shape:	Trapezium	
Shape spread:	(8x2)	
No. of half-side players (Neut):	5{(5(0)}	
No. of Outer players (Inner):	10 (0)	
No. of Mid-fielders (Neut):	0(0)	
No. of Att/Def Mid-fielders:	(0/0)	(0/0)

Three-Seven and Seven-Three

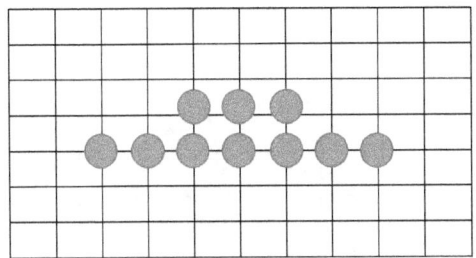

	Three-Seven	Seven-Three
Playing Orientation:	Defensive (7-3)	Attacking (3-7)
No. of Strikers /Def players:	(3/7)	(7/3)
Shape:	Trapezium	
Shape spread:	(7X2)	
No. of half-side players (Neut):	6{(4(2)}	
No. of Outer players (Inner):	10 (0)	
No. of Mid-fielders (Neut):	0(0)	
No. of Att/Def Mid-fielders:	(0/0)	(0/0)

Four-Six and Six-Four

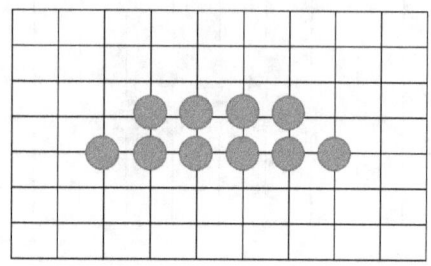

	Four-Six	Six-Four
Playing Orientation:	Defensive (6-4)	Attacking (4-6)
No. of Strikers/Def players:	(4/6)	(6/4)
Shape:	Trapezium	
Shape spread:	(6X2)	
No. of half-side players (Neut):	5{(5(0)}	
No. of Outer players (Inner):	10 (0)	
No. of Mid-fielders (Neut):	0(0)	
No. of Att/Def Mid-fielders:	(0/0)	(0/0)

Five-Five

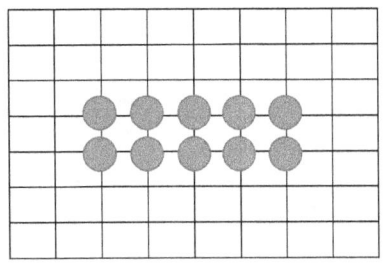

	Five-Five
Playing Orientation:	Neutral (5-5)
No. of Strikers/Def players:	(5/5)
Shape:	Rectangle
Shape spread:	(5X2)
No. of half-side players (Neut):	6{(4(2)}
No. of Outer players (Inner):	10 (0)
No. of Mid-fielders (Neut):	0(0)
No. of Att/Def Mid-fielders:	(0/0)

LEVEL 3

Formations: 36

Symmetrically neutral: 4

One-One-Eight and Eight-One-One

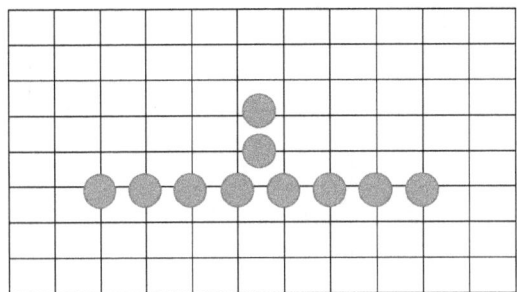

	One-One-Eight	Eight-One-One
Playing Orientation:	Defensive (9-2)	Attacking (2-9)
No. of Att/Def players:	(1/8)	(8/1)
Shape:	Triangle	
Shape spread:	(9X3)	
No. of half-side players (Neut):	6{(4(2)}	
No. of Outer players (Inner):	9 (1)	
No. of Mid-fielders (Neut):	1(1)	
No. of Att/Def Mid-fielders:	(0/0)	(0/0)

One-Two-Seven and Seven-Two-One

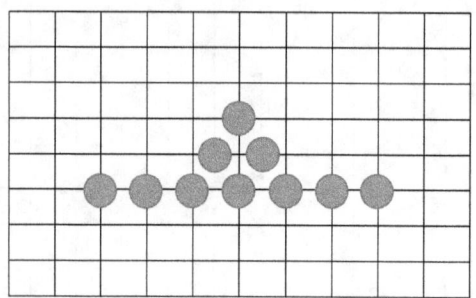

	One-Two-Seven	Seven-Two-One
Playing Orientation:	Defensive (9-3)	Attacking (3-9)
No. of Strikers/Def players:	(1/7)	(7/1)
Shape:	Triangle	
Shape spread:	(9X3)	
No. of half-side players (Neut):	6{(4(2)}	
No. of Outer players (Inner):	8 (2)	
No. of Mid-fielders (Neut):	2(2)	
No. of Att/Def Mid-fielders:	(0/0)	(0/0)

One-Three-Six and Six-Three-One

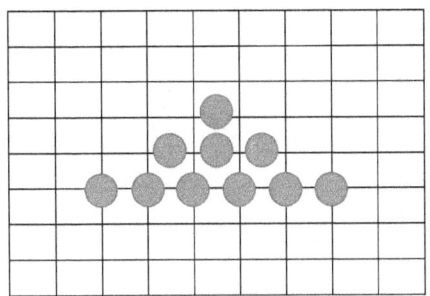

	One-Three-Six	Six-Three-One
Playing Orientation:	Defensive (9-4)	Attacking (4-9)
No. of Strikers/Def players:	(1/6)	(6/1)
Shape:	Triangle	
Shape spread:	(9X3)	
No. of half-side players (Neut):	6{(4(2)}	
No. of Outer players (Inner):	7 (3)	
No. of Mid-fielders (Neut):	3(3)	
No. of Att/Def Mid-fielders:	(0/0)	(0/0)

One-Four-Five and Five-Four-One

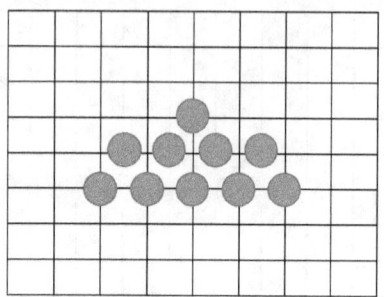

	One-Four-Five	Five-Four-One
Playing Orientation:	Defensive (9-5)	Attacking (5-9)
No. of Strikers/Def players:	(1/5)	(5/1)
Shape:	Pentagon	
Shape spread:	(9X3)	
No. of half-side players (Neut):	6{(4(2)}	
No. of Outer players (Inner):	8 (2)	
No. of Mid-fielders (Neut):	4(4)	
No. of Att/Def Mid-fielders:	(0/0)	(0/0)

One-Five-Four and Four-Five-One

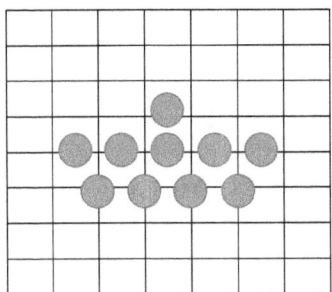

	One-Five-Four	Four-Five-One
Playing Orientation:	Defensive (9-6)	Attacking (6-9)
No. of Strikers/Def players:	(1/4)	(4/1)
Shape:	Pentagon	
Shape spread:	(9X3)	
No. of half-side players (Neut):	6{(4(2)}	
No. of Outer players (Inner):	7 (3)	
No. of Mid-fielders (Neut):	5(5)	
No. of Att/Def Mid-fielders:	(0/0)	(0/0)

One-Six-Three and Three-Six-One

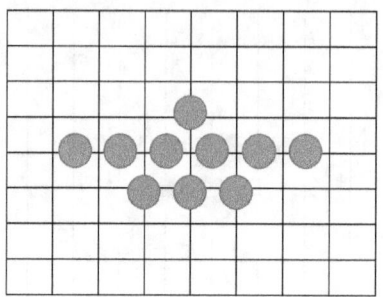

	One-Six-Three	Three-Six-One
Playing Orientation:	Defensive (9-7)	Attacking (7-9)
No. of Strikers/Def players:	(1/3)	(3/1)
Shape:	Pentagon	
Shape spread:	(9X3)	
No. of half-side players (Neut):	6{(4(2)}	
No. of Outer players (Inner):	6 (4)	
No. of Mid-fielders (Neut):	6(6)	
No. of Att/Def Mid-fielders:	(0/0)	(0/0)

One-Seven-Two and Two-Seven-One

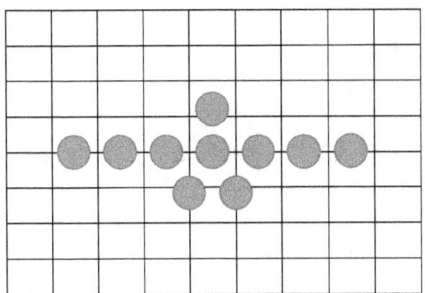

	One-Seven-Two	Two-Seven-One
Playing Orientation:	Defensive (9-8)	Attacking (8-9)
No. of Strikers/Def players:	(1/2)	(2/1)
Shape:	Pentagon	
Shape spread:	(9X3)	
No. of half-side players (Neut):	6{(4(2)}	
No. of Outer players (Inner):	5 (5)	
No. of Mid-fielders (Neut):	7(7)	
No. of Att/Def Mid-fielders:	(0/0)	(0/0)

One-Eight-One

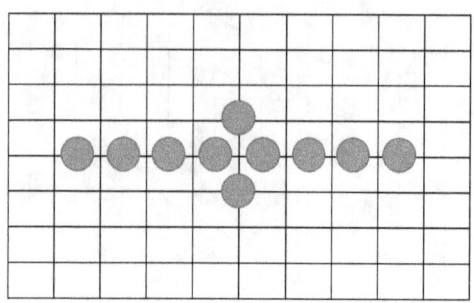

	One-Eight-One
Playing Orientation:	Neutral (9-9)
No. of Att/Def players:	(1/1)
Shape:	Quadrilateral
Shape spread:	(9X3)
No. of half-side players (Neut):	6{(4(2)}
No. of Outer players (Inner):	4(6)
No. of Mid-fielders (Neut):	8(8)
No. of Att/Def Mid-fielders:	(0/0)

Two-One-Seven and Seven-One-Two

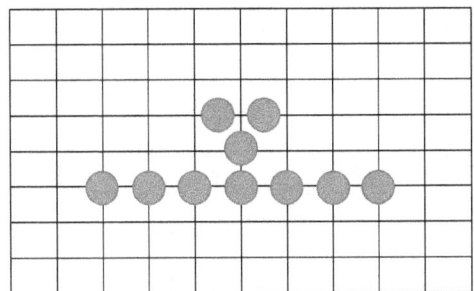

	Two-One-Seven	Seven-One-Two
Playing Orientation:	Defensive (8-3)	Attacking (3-8)
No. of Strikers/Def players:	(2/7)	(7/2)
Shape:	Trapezium	
Shape spread:	(9X3)	
No. of half-side players (Neut):	6{(4(2)}	
No. of Outer players (Inner):	9 (1)	
No. of Mid-fielders (Neut):	1(1)	
No. of Att/Def Mid-fielders:	(0/0)	(0/0)

Two-Two-Six and Six-Two-Two

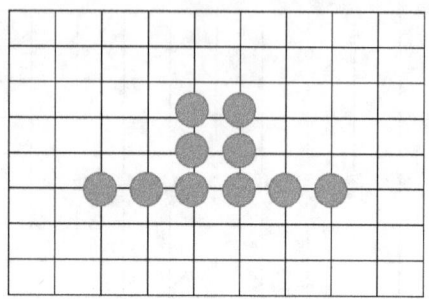

	Two-Two-Six	Six-Two-Two
Playing Orientation:	Defensive (8-4)	Attacking (4-8)
No. of Strikers/Def players:	(2/6)	(6/2)
Shape:	Trapezium	
Shape spread:	(6X3)	
No. of half-side players (Neut):	5{(5(0)}	
No. of Outer players (Inner):	8 (2)	
No. of Mid-fielders (Neut):	2(2)	
No. of Att/Def Mid-fielders:	(0/0)	(0/0)

Two-Three-Five and Five-Three-Two

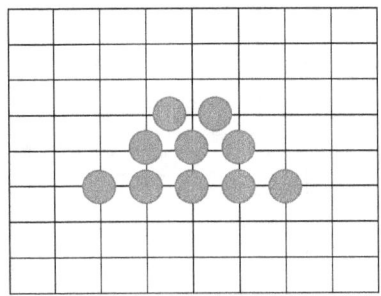

	Two-Three-Five	Five-Three-Two
Playing Orientation:	Defensive (8-5)	Attacking (5-8)
No. of Strikers/Def players:	(2/5)	(5/2)
Shape:	Trapezium	
Shape spread:	(7X3)	
No. of half-side players (Neut):	6{(4(2)}	
No. of Outer players (Inner):	7 (3)	
No. of Mid-fielders (Neut):	3(3)	
No. of Att/Def Mid-fielders:	(0/0)	(0/0)

Two-Four-Four and Four-Four-Two

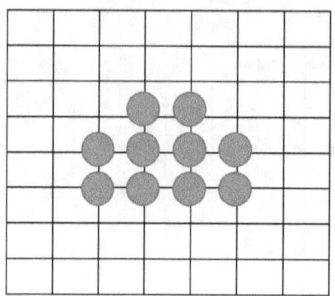

	Two-Four-Four	Four-Four-Two
Playing Orientation:	Defensive (8-6)	Attacking (6-8)
No. of Strikers/Def players:	(2/4)	(4/2)
Shape:	Hexagon	
Shape spread:	(4X3)	
No. of half-side players (Neut):	5{(5(0)}	
No. of Outer players (Inner):	8 (2)	
No. of Mid-fielders (Neut):	4(4)	
No. of Att/Def Mid-fielders:	(0/0)	(0/0)

Two-Five-Three and Three-Five-Two

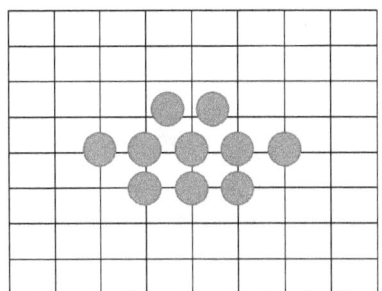

	Two-Five-Three	Three-Five-Two
Playing Orientation:	Defensive (8-7)	Attacking (7-8)
No. of Strikers/Def players:	(2/3)	(3/2)
Shape:	Hexagon	
Shape spread:	(7X3)	
No. of half-side players (Neut):	6{(4(2)}	
No. of Outer players (Inner):	7 (3)	
No. of Mid-fielders (Neut):	5(5)	
No. of Att/Def Mid-fielders:	(0/0)	(0/0)

Two-Six-Two

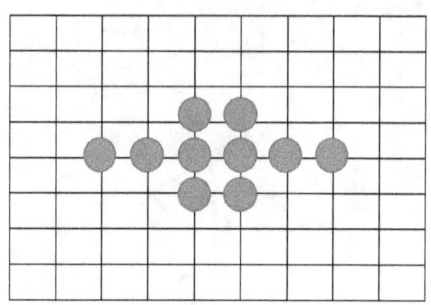

	Two-Six-Two
Playing Orientation:	Neutral (8-8)
No. of Strikers/Def players:	(2/2)
Shape:	Hexagon
Shape spread:	(6X3)
No. of half-side players (Neut):	5{(5(0)}
No. of Outer players (Inner):	6 (4)
No. of Mid-fielders (Neut):	6(6)
No. of Att/Def Mid-fielders:	(0/0)

Three-One-Six and Six-One-Three

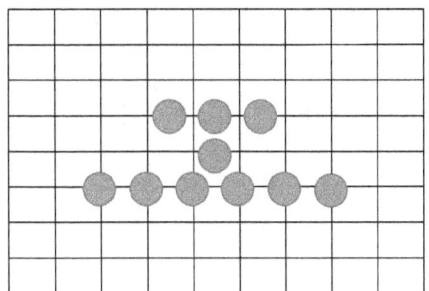

	Three-One-Six	Six-One-Three
Playing Orientation:	Defensive (7-4)	Attacking (4-7)
No. of Strikers/Def players:	(3/6)	(6/3)
Shape:	Trapezium	
Shape spread:	(9X3)	
No. of half-side players (Neut):	6{(4(2)}	
No. of Outer players (Inner):	9 (1)	
No. of Mid-fielders (Neut):	1(1)	
No. of Att/Def Mid-fielders:	(0/0)	(0/0)

Three-Two-Five and Five-Two-Three

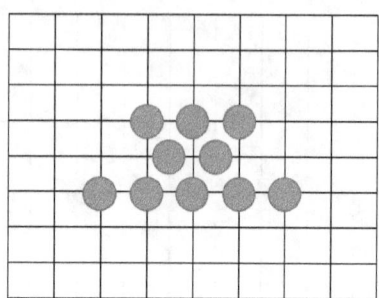

	Three-Two-Five	Five-Two-Three
Playing Orientation:	Defensive (7-5)	Attacking (5-7)
No. of Strikers/Def players:	(3/5)	(5/3)
Shape:	Trapezium	
Shape spread:	(7X3)	
No. of half-side players (Neut):	6{(4(2)}	
No. of Outer players (Inner):	8 (2)	
No. of Mid-fielders (Neut):	2(2)	
No. of Att/Def Mid-fielders:	(0/0)	(0/0)

Three-Three-Four and Four-Three-Three

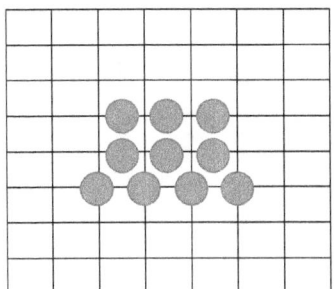

	Three-Three-Four	Four-Three-Three
Playing Orientation:	Defensive (7-6)	Attacking (6-7)
No. of Strikers/Def players:	(3/4)	(4/3)
Shape:	Trapezium	
Shape spread:	(7X3)	
No. of half-side players (Neut):	6{(4(2)}	
No. of Outer players (Inner):	7 (3)	
No. of Mid-fielders (Neut):	3(3)	
No. of Att/Def Mid-fielders:	(0/0)	(0/0)

Three-Four-Three

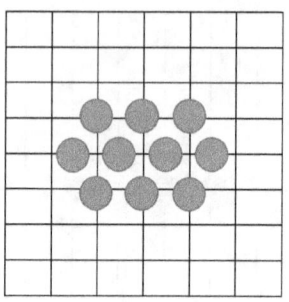

	Three-Four-Three
Playing Orientation:	Neutral (7-7)
No. of Strikers/Def players:	(3/3)
Shape:	Hexagon
Shape spread:	(7X3)
No. of half-side players (Neut):	6{(4(2)}
No. of Outer players (Inner):	8 (2)
No. of Mid-fielders (Neut):	4(4)
No. of Att/Def Mid-fielders:	(0/0)

Four-One-Five and Five-One-Four

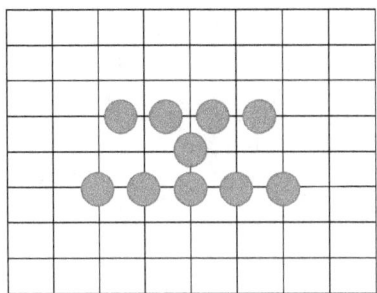

	Four-One-Five	Five-One-Four
Playing Orientation:	Defensive (6-5)	Attacking (5-6)
No. of Strikers/Def players:	(4/5)	(5/4)
Shape:	Trapezium	
Shape spread:	(9X3)	
No. of half-side players (Neut):	6{(4(2)}	
No. of Outer players (Inner):	9 (1)	
No. of Mid-fielders (Neut):	1(1)	
No. of Att/Def Mid-fielders:	(0/0)	(0/0)

Four-Two-Four

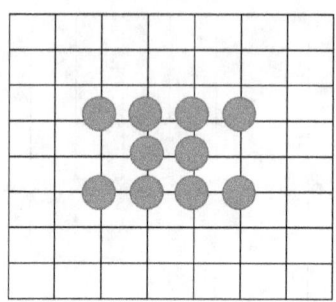

	Four-Two-Four
Playing Orientation:	Neutral (6-6)
No. of Strikers/Def players:	(4/4)
Shape:	Rectangle
Shape spread:	(4X3)
No. of half-side players (Neut):	5{(5(0)}
No. of Outer players (Inner):	8 (2)
No. of Mid-fielders (Neut):	2(2)
No. of Att/Def Mid-fielders:	(0/0)

LEVEL 4

Formations: 84

Symmetrically neutral: 4

One-One-One-Seven and Seven-One-One-One

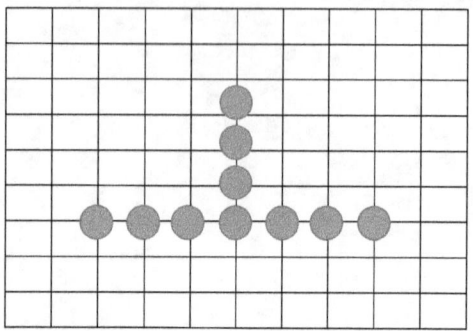

	One-One-One-Seven	Seven-One-One-One
Playing Orientation:	Defensive (8-2)	Attacking (2-8)
No. of Strikers/Def players:	(1/7)	(7/1)
Shape:	Triangle	
Shape spread:	(7X4)	
No. of half-side players (Neut):	7{(3(4)}	
No. of Outer players (Inner):	8 (2)	
No. of Mid-fielders (Neut):	2(0)	
No. of Att/Def Mid-fielders:	(1/1)	(1/1)

One-One-Two-Six and Six-Two-One-One

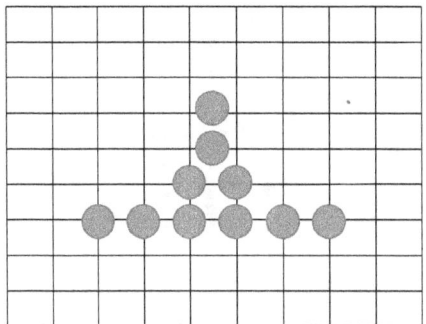

	One-One-Two-Six	Six-Two-One-One
Playing Orientation:	Defensive (8-2)	Attacking (2-8)
No. of Strikers/Def players:	(1/6)	(6/1)
Shape:	Triangle	
Shape spread:	(7X4)	
No. of half-side players (Neut):	6{(4(2)}	
No. of Outer players (Inner):	7 (3)	
No. of Mid-fielders (Neut):	3(0)	
No. of Att/Def Mid-fielders:	(1/2)	(2/1)

One-One-Three-Five and Five-Three-One-One

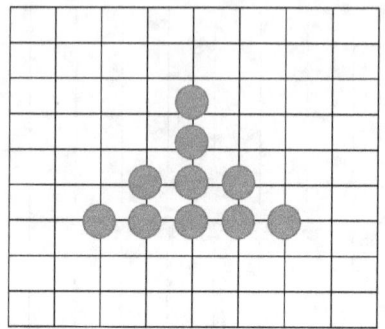

	One-One-Three-Five	Five-Three-One-One
Playing Orientation:	Defensive (8-2)	Attacking (2-8)
No. of Strikers/Def players:	(1/5)	(5/1)
Shape:	Triangle	
Shape spread:	(5X4)	
No. of half-side players (Neut):	7{(3(4)}	
No. of Outer players (Inner):	6 (4)	
No. of Mid-fielders (Neut):	4(0)	
No. of Att/Def Mid-fielders:	(1/3)	(3/1)

One-One-Four-Four and Four-Four-One-One

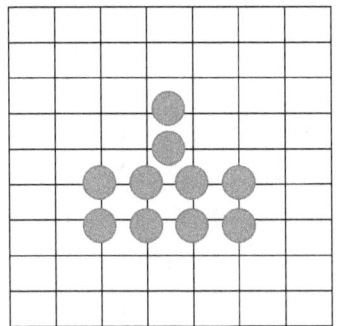

	One-One-Four-Four	Four-Four-One-One
Playing Orientation:	Defensive (8-2)	Attacking (2-8)
No. of Strikers/Def players:	(1/4)	(4/1)
Shape:	Pentagon	
Shape spread:	(5X4)	
No. of half-side players (Neut):	6{(4(2)}	
No. of Outer players (Inner):	7 (3)	
No. of Mid-fielders (Neut):	5(0)	
No. of Att/Def Mid-fielders:	(1/4)	(4/1)

One-One-Five-Three and Three-Five-One-One

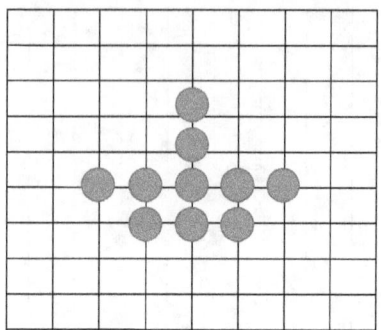

	One-One-Five-Three	Three-Five-One-One
Playing Orientation:	Defensive (8-2)	Attacking (2-8)
No. of Strikers/Def players:	(1/3)	(3/1)
Shape:	Pentagon	
Shape spread:	(5X4)	
No. of half-side players (Neut):	7{(3(4)}	
No. of Outer players (Inner):	6 (4)	
No. of Mid-fielders (Neut):	6(0)	
No. of Att/Def Mid-fielders:	(1/5)	(5/1)

One-One-Six-Two and Two-Six-One-One

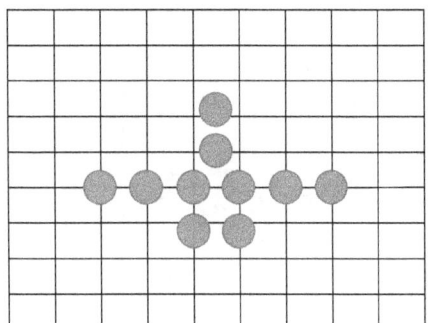

	One-One-Six-Two	Two-Six-One-One
Playing Orientation:	Defensive (8-2)	Attacking (2-8)
No. of Strikers/Def players:	(1/2)	(2/1)
Shape:	Pentagon	
Shape spread:	(7X4)	
No. of half-side players (Neut):	6{(4(2)}	
No. of Outer players (Inner):	5 (5)	
No. of Mid-fielders (Neut):	7(0)	
No. of Att/Def Mid-fielders:	(1/6)	(6/1)

One-One-Seven-One and One-Seven-One-One

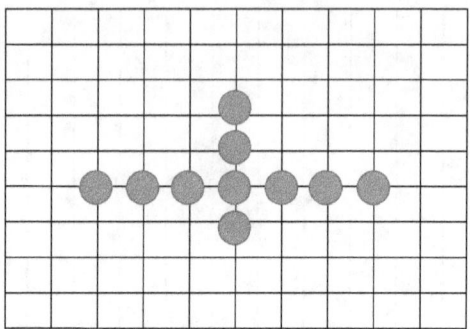

	One-One-Seven-One	One-Seven-One-One
Playing Orientation:	Defensive (8-2)	Attacking (2-8)
No. of Strikers/Def players:	(1/1)	(1/1)
Shape:	Quadrilateral	
Shape spread:	(7X4)	
No. of half-side players (Neut):	7{(3(4)}	
No. of Outer players (Inner):	4 (6)	
No. of Mid-fielders (Neut):	8(0)	
No. of Att/Def Mid-fielders:	(1/7)	(7/1)

One-Two-One-Six and Six-One-Two-One

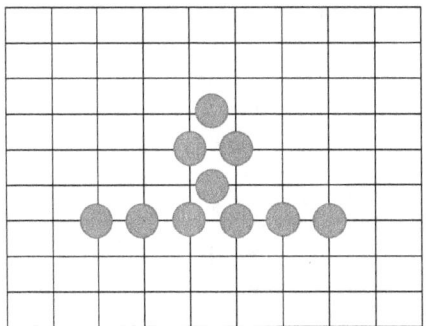

	One-Two-One-Six	Six-One-Two-One
Playing Orientation:	Defensive (7-3)	Attacking (3-7)
No. of Strikers/Def players:	(1/6)	(6/1)
Shape:	Triangle	
Shape spread:	(7X4)	
No. of half-side players (Neut):	6{(4(2)}	
No. of Outer players (Inner):	7 (3)	
No. of Mid-fielders (Neut):	3(0)	
No. of Att/Def Mid-fielders:	(2/1)	(1/2)

One-Two-Two-Five and Five-Two-Two-One

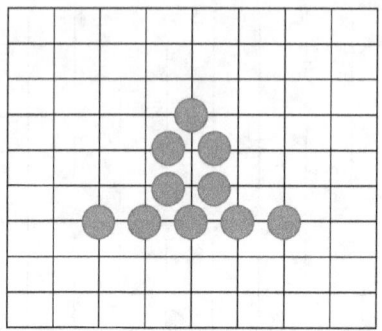

	One-Two-Two-Five	Five-Two-Two-One
Playing Orientation:	Defensive (7-3)	Attacking (3-7)
No. of Strikers/Def players:	(1/5)	(5/1)
Shape:	Triangle	
Shape spread:	(7X4)	
No. of half-side players (Neut):	6{(4(2)}	
No. of Outer players (Inner):	6 (4)	
No. of Mid-fielders (Neut):	4(0)	
No. of Att/Def Mid-fielders:	(2/2)	(2/2)

One-Two-Three-Four and Four-Three-Two-One

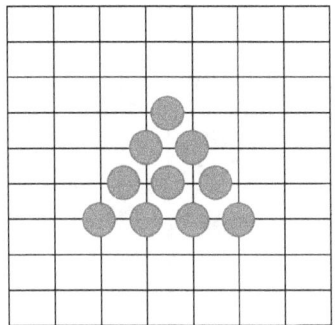

	One-Two-Three-Four	Four-Three-Two-One
Playing Orientation:	Defensive (7-3)	Attacking (3-7)
No. of Strikers/Def players:	(1/4)	(4/1)
Shape:	Triangle	
Shape spread:	(7X4)	
No. of half-side players (Neut):	6{(4(2)}	
No. of Outer players (Inner):	9 (1)	
No. of Mid-fielders (Neut):	5(0)	
No. of Att/Def Mid-fielders:	(2/3)	(3/2)

One-Two-Four-Three and Three-Four-Two-One

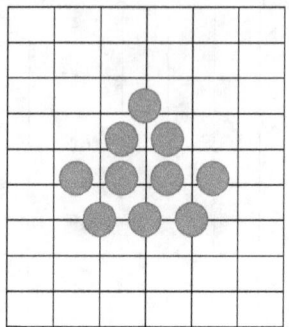

	One-Two-Four-Three	Three-Four-Two-One
Playing Orientation:	Defensive (7-3)	Attacking (3-7)
No. of Strikers/Def players:	(1/3)	(3/1)
Shape:	Pentagon	
Shape spread:	(7X4)	
No. of half-side players (Neut):	6{(4(2)}	
No. of Outer players (Inner):	6 (4)	
No. of Mid-fielders (Neut):	6(0)	
No. of Att/Def Mid-fielders:	(2/4)	(4/2)

One-Two-Five-Two and Two-Five-Two-One

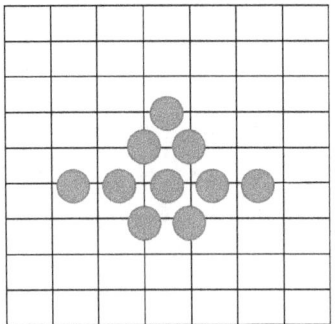

	One-Two-Five-Two	Two-Five-Two-One
Playing Orientation:	Defensive (7-3)	Attacking (3-7)
No. of Strikers/Def players:	(1/2)	(2/1)
Shape:	Pentagon	
Shape spread:	(7X4)	
No. of half-side players (Neut):	6{(4(2)}	
No. of Outer players (Inner):	5 (5)	
No. of Mid-fielders (Neut):	7(0)	
No. of Att/Def Mid-fielders:	(2/5)	(5/2)

One-Two-Six-One and One-Six-Two-One

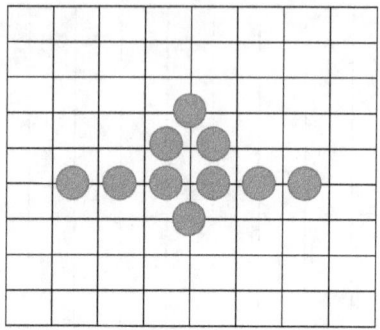

	One-Two-Six-One	One-Six-Two-One
Playing Orientation:	Defensive (7-3)	Attacking (3-7)
No. of Strikers/Def players:	(1/1)	(1/1)
Shape:	Quadrilateral	
Shape spread:	(7X4)	
No. of half-side players (Neut):	6{(4(2)}	
No. of Outer players (Inner):	4 (6)	
No. of Mid-fielders (Neut):	8(0)	
No. of Att/Def Mid-fielders:	(2/6)	(6/2)

One-Three-One-Five and Five-One-Three-One

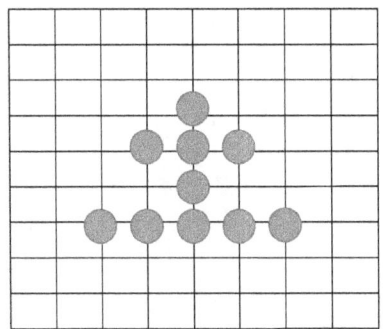

	One-Three-One-Five	Five-One-Three-One
Playing Orientation:	Defensive (6-4)	Attacking (4-6)
No. of Strikers/Def players:	(1/5)	(5/1)
Shape:	Pentagon	
Shape spread:	(5X4)	
No. of half-side players (Neut):	7{(3(4)}	
No. of Outer players (Inner):	8 (2)	
No. of Mid-fielders (Neut):	4(0)	
No. of Att/Def Mid-fielders:	(3/1)	(1/3)

One-Three-Two-Four and Four-Two-Three-One

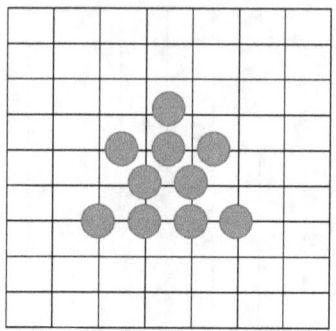

	One-Three-Two-Four	Four-Two-Three-One
Playing Orientation:	Defensive (6-4)	Attacking (4-6)
No. of Strikers/Def players:	(1/4)	(4/1)
Shape:	Pentagon	
Shape spread:	(7X4)	
No. of half-side players (Neut):	6{(4(2)}	
No. of Outer players (Inner):	7 (3)	
No. of Mid-fielders (Neut):	5(0)	
No. of Att/Def Mid-fielders:	(3/2)	(2/3)

One-Three-Three-Three and Three-Three-Three-One

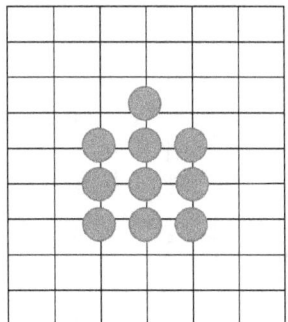

	One-Three-Three-Three	Three-Three-Three-One
Playing Orientation:	Defensive (6-4)	Attacking (4-6)
No. of Strikers/Def players:	(1/3)	(3/1)
Shape:	Pentagon	
Shape spread:	(3X4)	
No. of half-side players (Neut):	7{(3(4)}	
No. of Outer players (Inner):	8 (2)	
No. of Mid-fielders (Neut):	6(0)	
No. of Att/Def Mid-fielders:	(3/3)	(3/3)

One-Three-Four-Two and Two-Four-Three-One

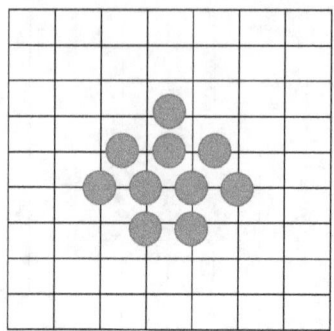

	One-Three-Four-Two	**Two-Four-Three-One**
Playing Orientation:	Defensive (6-4)	Attacking (4-6)
No. of Strikers/Def players:	(1/2)	(2/1)
Shape:	Heptagon	
Shape spread:	(7X4)	
No. of half-side players (Neut):	6{(4(2)}	
No. of Outer players (Inner):	7 (3)	
No. of Mid-fielders (Neut):	7(0)	
No. of Att/Def Mid-fielders:	(3/4)	(4/3)

One-Three-Five-One and One-Five-Three-One

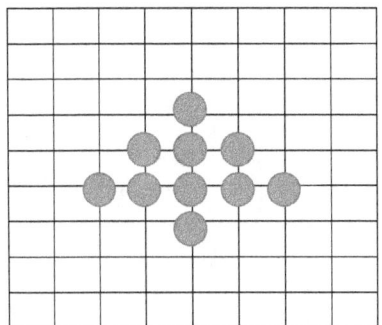

	One-Three-Five-One	One-Five-Three-One
Playing Orientation:	Defensive (6-4)	Attacking (4-6)
No. of Strikers/Def players:	(1/1)	(1/1)
Shape:	Quadrilateral	
Shape spread:	(5X4)	
No. of half-side players (Neut):	7{(3(4)}	
No. of Outer players (Inner):	6 (4)	
No. of Mid-fielders (Neut):	8(0)	
No. of Att/Def Mid-fielders:	(3/5)	(5/3)

One-Four-One-Four and Four-One-Four-One

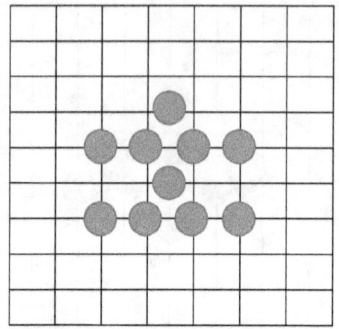

	One-Four-One-Four	Four-One-Four-One
Playing Orientation:	Neutral (5-5)	
No. of Strikers/Def players:	(1/4)	(4/1)
Shape:	Pentagon	
Shape spread:	(5X4)	
No. of half-side players (Neut):	6{(4(2)}	
No. of Outer players (Inner):	7 (3)	
No. of Mid-fielders (Neut):	5(0)	
No. of Att/Def Mid-fielders:	(4/1)	(1/4)

One-Four-Two-Three and Three-Two-Four-One

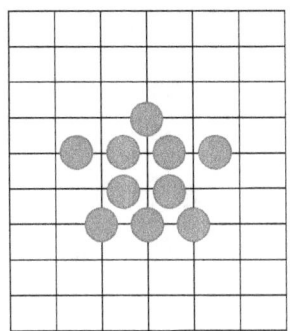

	One-Four-Two-Three	Three-Two-Four-One
Playing Orientation:	Neutral (5-5)	
No. of Strikers/Def players:	(1/3)	(3/1)
Shape:	Pentagon	
Shape spread:	(7X4)	
No. of half-side players (Neut):	6{(4(2)}	
No. of Outer players (Inner):	6 (4)	
No. of Mid-fielders (Neut):	6(0)	
No. of Att/Def Mid-fielders:	(4/2)	(2/4)

One-Four-Three-Two and Two-Three-Four-One

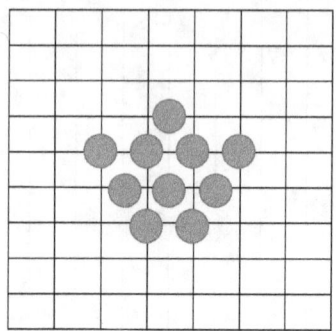

	One-Four-Three-Two	Two-Three-Four-One
Playing Orientation:	Neutral (5-5)	
No. of Strikers/Def players:	(1/2)	(2/1)
Shape:	Pentagon	
Shape spread:	(7X4)	
No. of half-side players (Neut):	6{(4(2)}	
No. of Outer players (Inner):	7 (3)	
No. of Mid-fielders (Neut):	7(0)	
No. of Att/Def Mid-fielders:	(4/3)	(3/4)

One-Four-Four-One

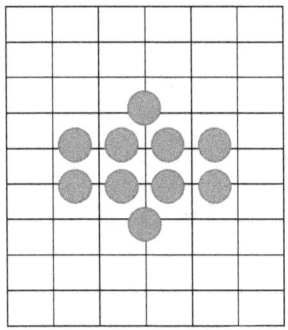

                                  One-Four-Four-One

Playing Orientation:	Neutral (5-5)
No. of Strikers/Def players:	(1/1)
Shape:	Hexagon
Shape spread:	(5X4)
No. of half-side players (Neut):	6{(4(2)}
No. of Outer players (Inner):	6 (4)
No. of Mid-fielders (Neut):	8(0)
No. of Att/Def Mid-fielders:	(4/4)

One-Five-One-Three and Three-One-Five-One

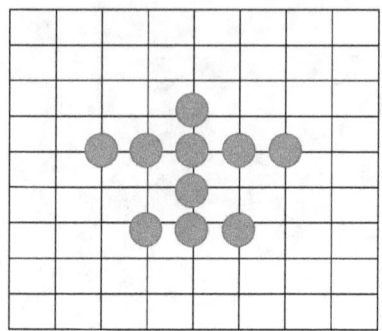

	One-Five-One-Three	Three-One-Five-One
Playing Orientation:	Attacking (4-6)	Defensive (6-4)
No. of Strikers/Def players:	(1/3)	(3/1)
Shape:	Pentagon	
Shape spread:	(5X4)	
No. of half-side players (Neut):	7{(3(4)}	
No. of Outer players (Inner):	6 (4)	
No. of Mid-fielders (Neut):	6(0)	
No. of Att/Def Mid-fielders:	(5/1)	(1/5)

One-Five-Two-Two and Two-Two-Five-One

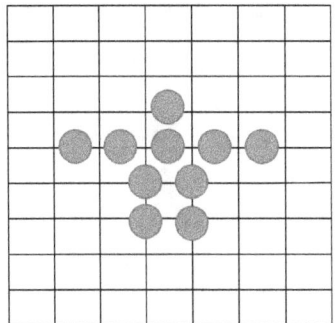

	One-Five-Two-Two	Two-Two-Five-One
Playing Orientation:	Attacking (4-6)	Defensive (6-4)
No. of Strikers/Def players:	(1/2)	(2/1)
Shape:	Pentagon	
Shape spread:	(7X4)	
No. of half-side players (Neut):	6{(4(2)}	
No. of Outer players (Inner):	5 (5)	
No. of Mid-fielders (Neut):	7(0)	
No. of Att/Def Mid-fielders:	(5/2)	(2/5)

One-Six-One-Two and Two-One-Six-One

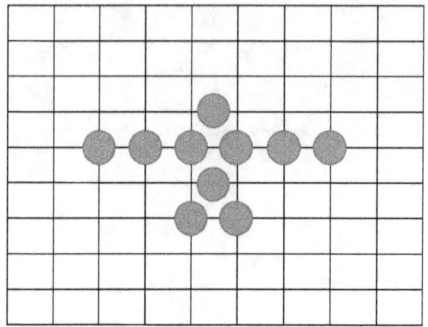

	One-Six-One-Two	Two-One-Six-One
Playing Orientation:	Attacking (3-7)	Defensive (7-3)
No. of Strikers/Def players:	(1/2)	(2/1)
Shape:	Pentagon	
Shape spread:	(7X4)	
No. of half-side players (Neut):	6{(4(2)}	
No. of Outer players (Inner):	5 (5)	
No. of Mid-fielders (Neut):	7(0)	
No. of Att/Def Mid-fielders:	(6/1)	(1/6)

Two-One-One-Six and Six-One-One-Two

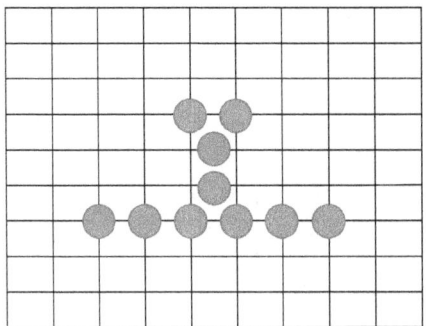

	Two-One-One-Six	Six-One-One-Two
Playing Orientation:	Defensive (7-3)	Attacking (3-7)
No. of Strikers/Def players:	(2/6)	(6/2)
Shape:	Trapezium	
Shape spread:	(7X4)	
No. of half-side players (Neut):	6{(4(2)}	
No. of Outer players (Inner):	8 (2)	
No. of Mid-fielders (Neut):	2(0)	
No. of Att/Def Mid-fielders:	(1/1)	(1/1)

Two-One-Two-Five and Five-Two-One-Two

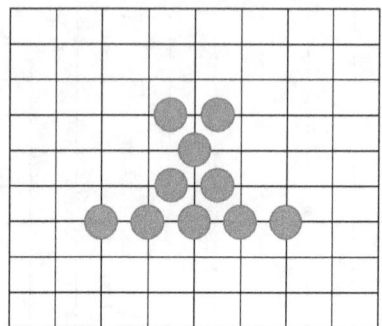

	Two-One-Two-Five	Five-Two-One-Two
Playing Orientation:	Defensive (7-3)	Attacking (3-7)
No. of Strikers/Def players:	(2/5)	(5/2)
Shape:	Trapezium	
Shape spread:	(7X4)	
No. of half-side players (Neut):	6{(4(2)}	
No. of Outer players (Inner):	7 (3)	
No. of Mid-fielders (Neut):	3(0)	
No. of Att/Def Mid-fielders:	(1/2)	(2/1)

Two-One-Three-Four and Four-Three-One-Two

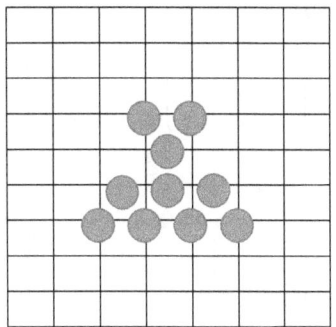

	Two-One-Three-Four	Four-Three-One-Two
Playing Orientation:	Defensive (7-3)	Attacking (3-7)
No. of Strikers/Def players:	(2/4)	(4/2)
Shape:	Trapezium	
Shape spread:	(7X4)	
No. of half-side players (Neut):	6{(4(2)}	
No. of Outer players (Inner):	6 (4)	
No. of Mid-fielders (Neut):	4(0)	
No. of Att/Def Mid-fielders:	(1/3)	(3/1)

Two-One-Four-Three and Three-Four-One-Two

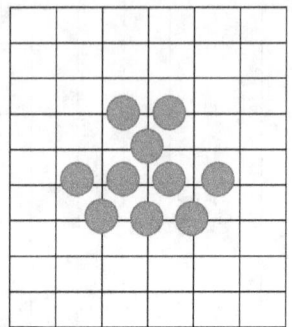

	Two-One-Four-Three	Three-Four-One-Two
Playing Orientation:	Defensive (7-3)	Attacking (3-7)
No. of Strikers/Def players:	(2/3)	(3/2)
Shape:	Hexagon	
Shape spread:	(7X4)	
No. of half-side players (Neut):	6{(4(2)}	
No. of Outer players (Inner):	7 (3)	
No. of Mid-fielders (Neut):	5(0)	
No. of Att/Def Mid-fielders:	(1/4)	(4/1)

Two-One-Five-Two and Two-Five-One-Two

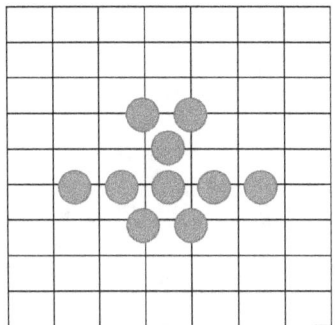

	Two-One-Five-Two	Two-Five-One-Two
Playing Orientation:	Defensive (7-3)	Attacking (3-7)
No. of Strikers/Def players:	(2/2)	(2/2)
Shape:	Hexagon	
Shape spread:	(7X4)	
No. of half-side players (Neut):	6{(4(2)}	
No. of Outer players (Inner):	6 (4)	
No. of Mid-fielders (Neut):	6(0)	
No. of Att/Def Mid-fielders:	(1/5)	(5/1)

Two-Two-One-Five and Five-One-Two-Two

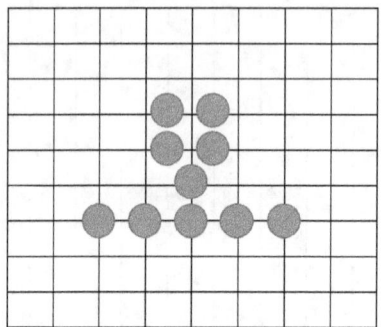

	Two-Two-One-Five	Five-One-Two-Two
Playing Orientation:	Defensive (6-4)	Attacking (4-6)
No. of Strikers/Def players:	(2/5)	(5/2)
Shape:	Trapezium	
Shape spread:	(7X4)	
No. of half-side players (Neut):	6{(4(2)}	
No. of Outer players (Inner):	7 (3)	
No. of Mid-fielders (Neut):	3(0)	
No. of Att/Def Mid-fielders:	(2/1)	(1/2)

Two-Two-Two-Four and Four-Two-Two-Two

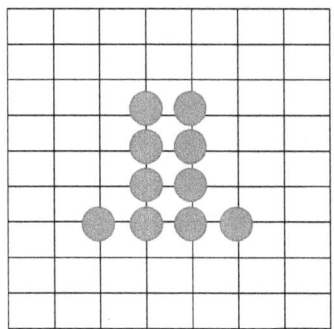

	Two-Two-Two-Four	Four-Two-Two-Two
Playing Orientation:	Defensive (6-4)	Attacking (4-6)
No. of Strikers/Def players:	(2/4)	(4/2)
Shape:	Trapezium	
Shape spread:	(4X4)	
No. of half-side players (Neut):	5{(5(0)}	
No. of Outer players (Inner):	6 (4)	
No. of Mid-fielders (Neut):	4(0)	
No. of Att/Def Mid-fielders:	(2/2)	(2/2)

Two-Two-Three-Three and Three-Three-Two-Two

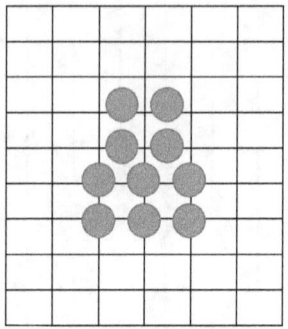

	Two-Two-Three-Three	Three-Three-Two-Two
Playing Orientation:	Defensive (6-4)	Attacking (4-6)
No. of Strikers/Def players:	(2/3)	(3/2)
Shape:	Hexagon	
Shape spread:	(5X4)	
No. of half-side players (Neut):	6{(4(2)}	
No. of Outer players (Inner):	7 (3)	
No. of Mid-fielders (Neut):	5(0)	
No. of Att/Def Mid-fielders:	(2/3)	(3/2)

Two-Three-One-Four and Four-One-Three-Two

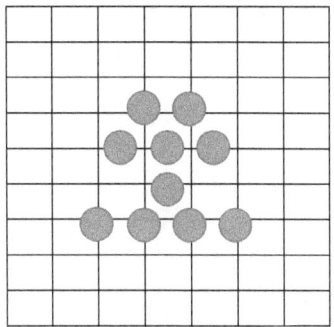

	Two-Three-One-Four	Four-One-Three-Two
Playing Orientation:	Neutral (5-5)	
No. of Strikers/Def players:	(2/4)	(4/2)
Shape:	Hexagon	
Shape spread:	(7X4)	
No. of half-side players (Neut):	6{(4(2)}	
No. of Outer players (Inner):	8 (2)	
No. of Mid-fielders (Neut):	4(0)	
No. of Att/Def Mid-fielders:	(3/1)	(1/3)

Two-Three-Two-Three and Three-Two-Three-Two

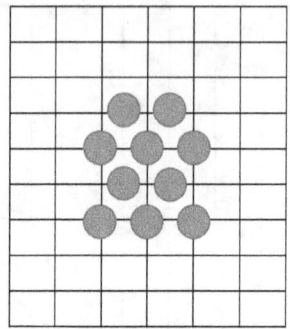

	Two-Three-Two-Three	Three-Two-Three-Two
Playing Orientation:	Neutral (5-5)	
No. of Strikers/Def players:	(2/3)	(3/2)
Shape:	Hexagon	
Shape spread:	(5X4)	
No. of half-side players (Neut):	6{(4(2)}	
No. of Outer players (Inner):	7 (3)	
No. of Mid-fielders (Neut):	5(0)	
No. of Att/Def Mid-fielders:	(3/2)	(2/3)

Two-Three-Three-Two

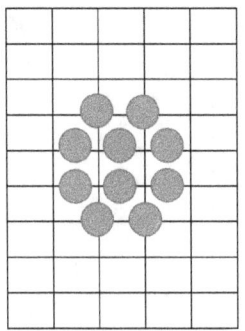

Two-Three-Three-Two

Playing Orientation:	Neutral (5-5)
No. of Strikers/Def players:	(2/2)
Shape:	Octagon
Shape spread:	(5X4)
No. of half-side players (Neut):	6{(4(2)}
No. of Outer players (Inner):	8 (2)
No. of Mid-fielders (Neut):	6(0)
No. of Att/Def Mid-fielders:	(3/3)

Two-Four-One-Three and Three-One-Four-Two

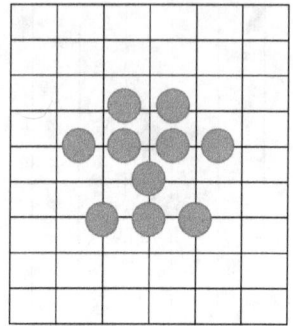

	Two-Four-One-Three	Three-One-Four-Two
Playing Orientation:	Attacking (4-6)	Defensive (6-4)
No. of Strikers /Def players:	(2/3)	(3/2)
Shape:	Hexagon	
Shape spread:	(7X4)	
No. of half-side players (Neut):	6{(4(2)}	
No. of Outer players (Inner):	7 (3)	
No. of Mid-fielders (Neut):	5(0)	
No. of Att/Def Mid-fielders:	(4/1)	(1/4)

Two-Four-Two-Two and Two-Two-Four-Two

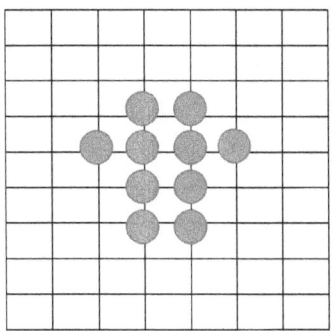

	Two-Four-Two-Two	Two-Two-Four-Two
Playing Orientation:	Attacking (4-6)	Defensive (6-4)
No. of Strikers /Def players:	(2/2)	(2/2)
Shape:	Hexagon	
Shape spread:	(4X4)	
No. of half-side players (Neut):	5{(5(0)}	
No. of Outer players (Inner):	6 (4)	
No. of Mid-fielders (Neut):	6(0)	
No. of Att/Def Mid-fielders:	(4/2)	(2/4)

Three-One-One-Five and Five-One-One-Three

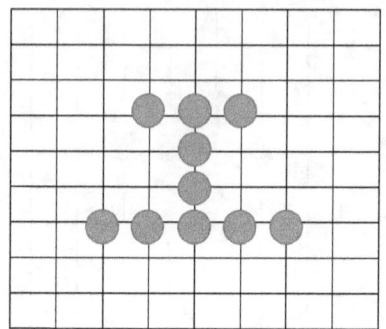

	Three-One-One-Five	Five-One-One-Three
Playing Orientation:	Defensive (6-4)	Attacking (4-6)
No. of Strikers /Def players:	(3/5)	(5/3)
Shape:	Trapezium	
Shape spread:	(5X4)	
No. of half-side players (Neut):	7{(3(4)}	
No. of Outer players (Inner):	8 (2)	
No. of Mid-fielders (Neut):	2(0)	
No. of Att/Def Mid-fielders:	(1/1)	(1/1)

Three-One-Two-Four and Four-Two-One-Three

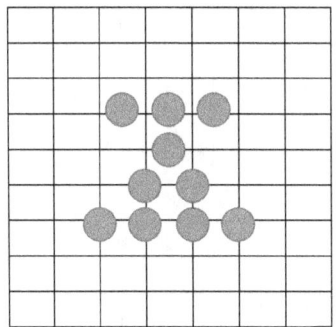

	Three-One-Two-Four	Four-Two-One-Three
Playing Orientation:	Defensive (6-4)	Attacking (4-6)
No. of Strikers /Def players:	(3/4)	(4/3)
Shape:	Trapezium	
Shape spread:	(7X4)	
No. of half-side players (Neut):	6{(4(2)}	
No. of Outer players (Inner):	7 (3)	
No. of Mid-fielders (Neut):	3(0)	
No. of Att/Def Mid-fielders:	(1/2)	(2/1)

Three-One-Three-Three and Three-Three-One-Three

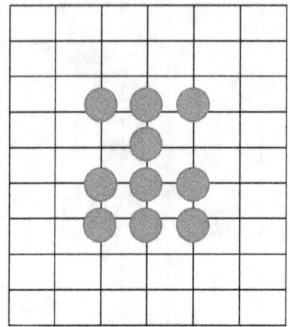

	Three-One-Three-Three	Three-Three-One-Three
Playing Orientation:	Defensive (6-4)	Attacking (4-6)
No. of Strikers /Def players:	(3/3)	(3/3)
Shape:	Rectangle	
Shape spread:	(3X4)	
No. of half-side players (Neut):	7{(3(4)}	
No. of Outer players (Inner):	8 (2)	
No. of Mid-fielders (Neut):	4(0)	
No. of Att/Def Mid-fielders:	(1/3)	(3/1)

Three-Two-One-Four and Four-One-Two-Three

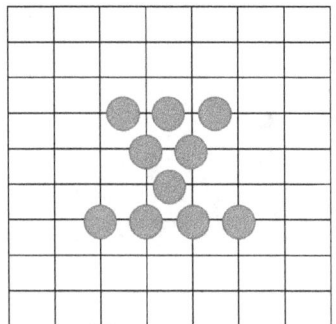

	Three-Two-One-Four	Four-One-Two-Three
Playing Orientation:	Neutral (5-5)	
No. of Strikers /Def players:	(3/4)	(4/3)
Shape:	Trapezium	
Shape spread:	(7X4)	
No. of half-side players (Neut):	6{(4(2)}	
No. of Outer players (Inner):	7 (3)	
No. of Mid-fielders (Neut):	3(0)	
No. of Att/Def Mid-fielders:	(2/1)	(1/2)

Three-Two-Two-Three

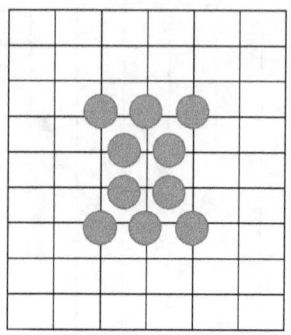

Three-Two-Two-Three

Playing Orientation:	Neutral (5-5)
No. of Strikers /Def players:	(3/3)
Shape:	Rectangle
Shape spread:	(5X4)
No. of half-side players (Neut):	6{(4(2)}
No. of Outer players (Inner):	6 (4)
No. of Mid-fielders (Neut):	4(0)
No. of Att/Def Mid-fielders:	(2/2)

Four-One-One-Four

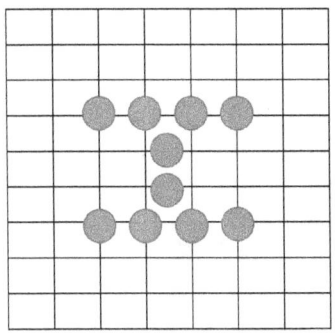

Four-One-One-Four

Playing Orientation:	Neutral (5-5)
No. of Strikers /Def players:	(4/4)
Shape:	Rectangle
Shape spread:	(5X4)
No. of half-side players (Neut):	6{(4(2)}
No. of Outer players (Inner):	8 (2)
No. of Mid-fielders (Neut):	2(0)
No. of Att/Def Mid-fielders:	(1/1)

LEVEL 5

Formations: 126

Symmetrically neutral: 6

One-One-One-One-Six and Six-One-One-One-One

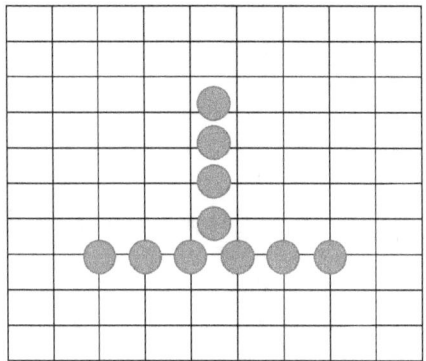

	One-One-One-One-Six	Six-One-One-One-One
Playing Orientation:	Defensive (8-3)	Attacking (3-8)
No. of Strikers /Def players:	(1/6)	(6/1)
Shape:	Triangle	
Shape spread:	(7X5)	
No. of half-side players (Neut):	7{(3(4)}	
No. of Outer players (Inner):	7 (3)	
No. of Mid-fielders (Neut):	3(1)	
No. of Att/Def Mid-fielders:	(1/1)	(1/1)

One-One-One-Two-Five and Five-Two-One-One-One

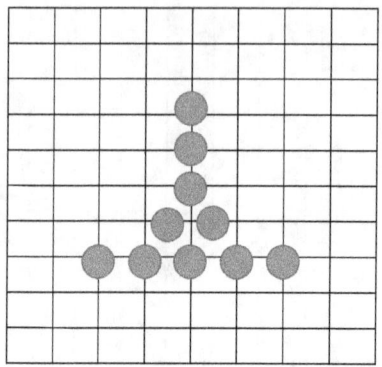

	One-One-One-Two-Five	Five-Two-One-One-One
Playing Orientation:	Defensive (8-3)	Attacking (3-8)
No. of Strikers /Def players:	(1/5)	(5/1)
Shape:	Triangle	
Shape spread:	(7X5)	
No. of half-side players (Neut):	7{(3(4)}	
No. of Outer players (Inner):	6 (4)	
No. of Mid-fielders (Neut):	4(1)	
No. of Att/Def Mid-fielders:	(1/2)	(2/1)

One-One-One-Three-Four and Four-Three-One-One-One

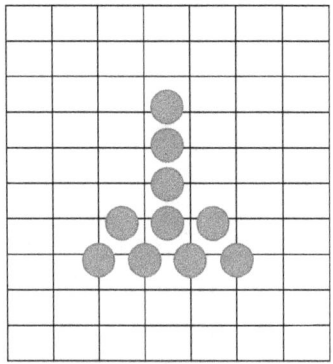

	One-One-One-Three-Four	Four-Three-One-One-One
Playing Orientation:	Defensive (8-3)	Attacking (3-8)
No. of Strikers /Def players:	(1/4)	(4/1)
Shape:	Triangle	
Shape spread:	(7X5)	
No. of half-side players (Neut):	7{(3(4)}	
No. of Outer players (Inner):	5 (5)	
No. of Mid-fielders (Neut):	5(1)	
No. of Att/Def Mid-fielders:	(1/3)	(3/1)

One-One-One-Four-Three and Three-Four-One-One-One

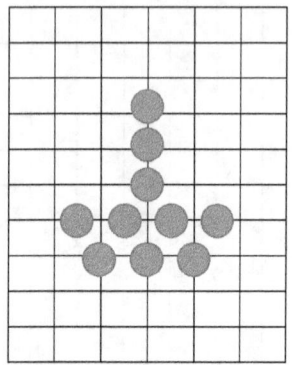

	One-One-One-Four-Three	Three-Four-One-One-One
Playing Orientation:	Defensive (8-3)	Attacking (3-8)
No. of Strikers /Def players:	(1/3)	(3/1)
Shape:	Pentagon	
Shape spread:	(7X5)	
No. of half-side players (Neut):	7{(3(4)}	
No. of Outer players (Inner):	6 (4)	
No. of Mid-fielders (Neut):	6(1)	
No. of Att/Def Mid-fielders:	(1/4)	(4/1)

One-One-One-Five-Two and Two-Five-One-One-One

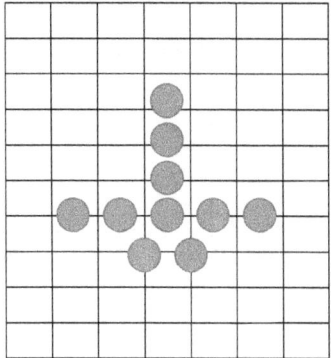

	One-One-One-Five-Two	Two-Five-One-One-One
Playing Orientation:	Defensive (8-3)	Attacking (3-8)
No. of Strikers /Def players:	(1/2)	(2/1)
Shape:	Pentagon	
Shape spread:	(7X5)	
No. of half-side players (Neut):	7{(3(4)}	
No. of Outer players (Inner):	5 (5)	
No. of Mid-fielders (Neut):	7(1)	
No. of Att/Def Mid-fielders:	(1/5)	(5/1)

One-One-One-Six-One and One-Six-One-One-One

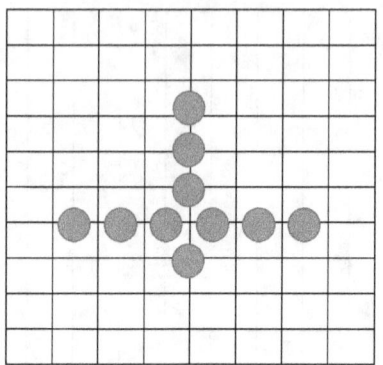

	One-One-One-Six-One	One-Six-One-One-One
Playing Orientation:	Defensive (8-3)	Attacking (3-8)
No. of Strikers /Def players:	(1/1)	(1/1)
Shape:	Quadrilateral	
Shape spread:	(7X5)	
No. of half-side players (Neut):	7{(3(4)}	
No. of Outer players (Inner):	4 (6)	
No. of Mid-fielders (Neut):	8(1)	
No. of Att/Def Mid-fielders:	(1/6)	(6/1)

One-One-Two-One-Five and Five-One-Two-One-One

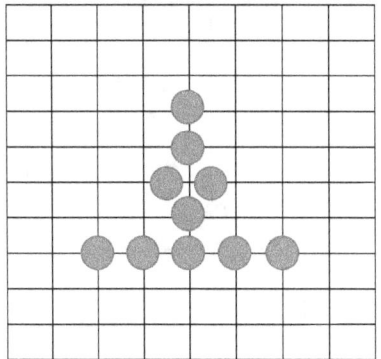

	One-One-Two-One-Five	Five-One-Two-One-One
Playing Orientation:	Defensive (8-4)	Attacking (4-8)
No. of Strikers /Def players:	(1/5)	(5/1)
Shape:	Triangle	
Shape spread:	(7X5)	
No. of half-side players (Neut):	7{(3(4)}	
No. of Outer players (Inner):	6 (4)	
No. of Mid-fielders (Neut):	4(2)	
No. of Att/Def Mid-fielders:	(1/1)	(1/1)

One-One-Two-Two-Four and Four-Two-Two-One-One

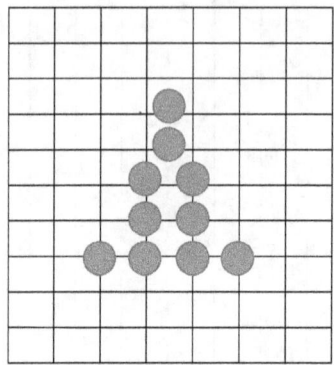

	One-One-Two-Two-Four	Four-Two-Two-One-One
Playing Orientation:	Defensive (8-4)	Attacking (4-8)
No. of Strikers /Def players:	(1/4)	(4/1)
Shape:	Triangle	
Shape spread:	(5X5)	
No. of half-side players (Neut):	6{(4(2)}	
No. of Outer players (Inner):	5 (5)	
No. of Mid-fielders (Neut):	5(2)	
No. of Att/Def Mid-fielders:	(1/2)	(2/1)

One-One-Two-Three-Three and Three-Three-Two-One-One

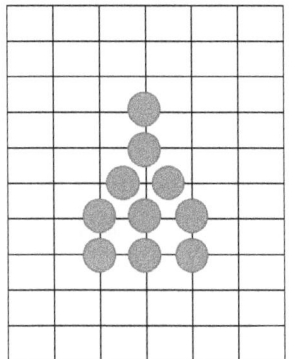

	One-One-Two-Three-Three	Three-Three-Two-One-One
Playing Orientation:	Defensive (8-4)	Attacking (4-8)
No. of Strikers /Def players:	(1/3)	(3/1)
Shape:	Pentagon	
Shape spread:	(5X5)	
No. of half-side players (Neut):	7{(3(4)}	
No. of Outer players (Inner):	6 (4)	
No. of Mid-fielders (Neut):	6(2)	
No. of Att/Def Mid-fielders:	(1/3)	(3/1)

One-One-Two-Five-One and One-Five-Two-One-One

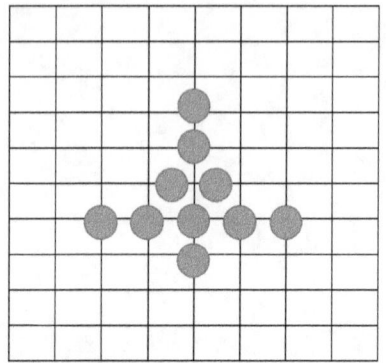

	One-One-Two-Five-One	One-Five-Two-One-One
Playing Orientation:	Defensive (8-4)	Attacking (4-8)
No. of Strikers /Def players:	(1/1)	(1/1)
Shape:	Quadrilateral	
Shape spread:	(7X5)	
No. of half-side players (Neut):	7{(3(4)}	
No. of Outer players (Inner):	4 (6)	
No. of Mid-fielders (Neut):	8(2)	
No. of Att/Def Mid-fielders:	(1/5)	(5/1)

One-One-Three-One-Four and Four-One-Three-One-One

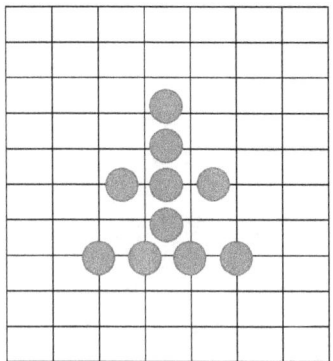

	One-One-Three-One-Four	Four-One-Three-One-One
Playing Orientation:	Defensive (8-5)	Attacking (5-8)
No. of Strikers /Def players:	(1/4)	(4/1)
Shape:	Pentagon	
Shape spread:	(7X5)	
No. of half-side players (Neut):	7{(3(4)}	
No. of Outer players (Inner):	7 (3)	
No. of Mid-fielders (Neut):	5(3)	
No. of Att/Def Mid-fielders:	(1/1)	(1/1)

One-One-Three-Two-Three and Three-Two-Three-One-One

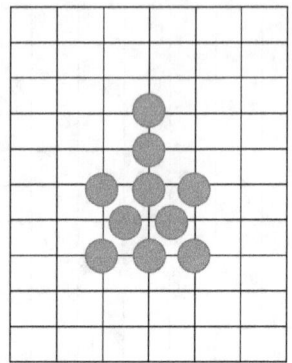

	One-One-Three-Two-Three	Three-Two-Three-One-One
Playing Orientation:	Defensive (8-5)	Attacking (5-8)
No. of Strikers /Def players:	(1/3)	(3/1)
Shape:	Pentagon	
Shape spread:	(5X5)	
No. of half-side players (Neut):	7{(3(4)}	
No. of Outer players (Inner):	6 (4)	
No. of Mid-fielders (Neut):	6(3)	
No. of Att/Def Mid-fielders:	(1/2)	(2/1)

One-One-Three-Three-Two and Two-Three-Three-One-One

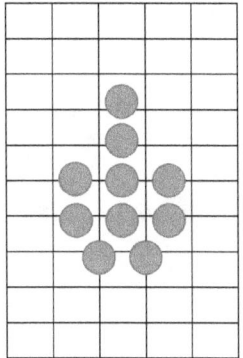

	One-One-Three-Three-Two	Two-Three-Three-One-One
Playing Orientation:	Defensive (8-5)	Attacking (5-8)
No. of Strikers /Def players:	(1/2)	(2/1)
Shape:	Heptagon	
Shape spread:	(5X5)	
No. of half-side players (Neut):	7{(3(4)}	
No. of Outer players (Inner):	7 (3)	
No. of Mid-fielders (Neut):	7(3)	
No. of Att/Def Mid-fielders:	(1/3)	(3/1)

One-One-Three-Four-One and One-Four-Three-One-One

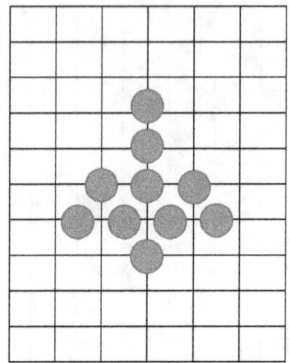

	One-One-Three-Four-One	One-Four-Three-One-One
Playing Orientation:	Defensive (8-5)	Attacking (5-8)
No. of Strikers /Def players:	(1/1)	(1/1)
Shape:	Hexagon	
Shape spread:	(7X5)	
No. of half-side players (Neut):	7{(3(4)}	
No. of Outer players (Inner):	6 (4)	
No. of Mid-fielders (Neut):	8(3)	
No. of Att/Def Mid-fielders:	(1/4)	(4/1)

One-One-Four-One-Three and Three-One-Four-One-One

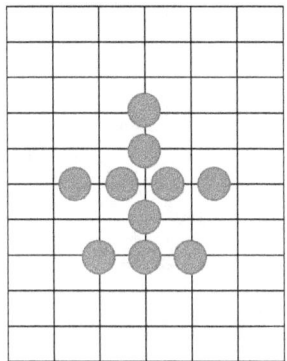

	One-One-Four-One-Three	Three-One-Four-One-One
Number of Inner players:	Defensive (8-6)	Attacking (6-8)
No. of Strikers /Def players:	(1/3)	(3/1)
Shape:	Pentagon	
Shape spread:	(7X5)	
No. of half-side players (Neut):	7{(3(4)}	
No. of Outer players (Inner):	6 (4)	
No. of Mid-fielders (Neut):	6(4)	
No. of Att/Def Mid-fielders:	(1/1)	(1/1)

One-One-Four-Two-Two and Two-Two-Four-One-One

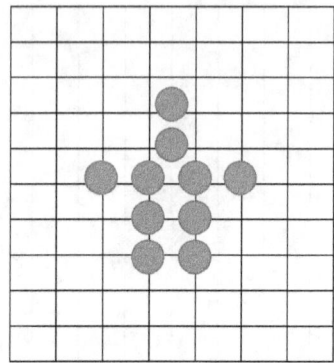

	One-One-Four-Two-Two	Two-Two-Four-One-One
Playing Orientation:	Defensive (8-6)	Attacking (6-8)
No. of Strikers /Def players:	(1/2)	(2/1)
Shape:	Pentagon	
Shape spread:	(5X5)	
No. of half-side players (Neut):	6{(4(2)}	
No. of Outer players (Inner):	5 (5)	
No. of Mid-fielders (Neut):	7(4)	
No. of Att/Def Mid-fielders:	(1/2)	(2/1)

One-One-Four-Three-One and One-Three-Four-One-One

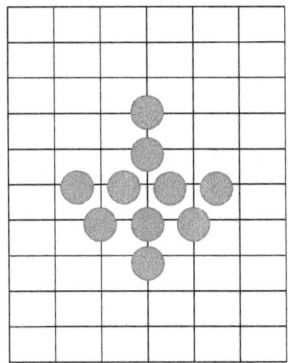

	One-One-Four-Three-One	One-Three-Four-One-One
Playing Orientation:	Defensive (8-6)	Attacking (6-8)
No. of Strikers /Def players:	(1/1)	(1/1)
Shape:	Hexagon	
Shape spread:	(7X5)	
No. of half-side players (Neut):	7{(3(4)}	
No. of Outer players (Inner):	6 (4)	
No. of Mid-fielders (Neut):	8(4)	
No. of Att/Def Mid-fielders:	(1/3)	(3/1)

One-One-Five-One-Two and Two-One-Five-One-One

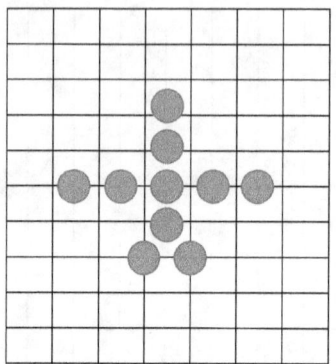

	One-One-Five-One-Two	Two-One-Five-One-One
Playing Orientation:	Defensive (8-7)	Attacking (7-8)
No. of Strikers /Def players:	(1/2)	(2/1)
Shape:	Pentagon	
Shape spread:	(7X5)	
No. of half-side players (Neut):	7{(3(4)}	
No. of Outer players (Inner):	5 (5)	
No. of Mid-fielders (Neut):	7(5)	
No. of Att/Def Mid-fielders:	(1/1)	(1/1)

One-One-Five-Two-One and One-Two-Five-One-One

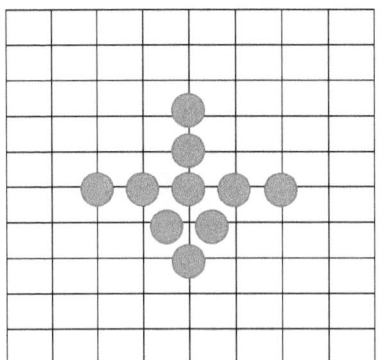

	One-One-Five-Two-One	One-Two-Five-One-One
Playing Orientation:	Defensive (8-7)	Attacking (7-8)
No. of Strikers /Def players:	(1/1)	(1/1)
Shape:	Quadrilateral	
Shape spread:	(7X5)	
No. of half-side players (Neut):	7{(3(4)}	
No. of Outer players (Inner):	4 (6)	
No. of Mid-fielders (Neut):	8(5)	
No. of Att/Def Mid-fielders:	(1/2)	(2/1)

One-One-Six-One-One

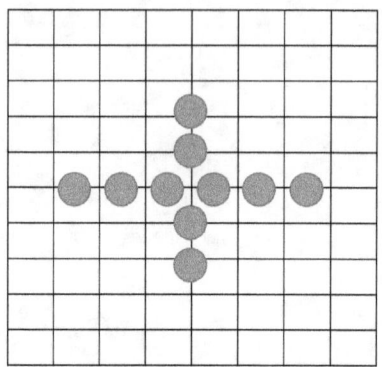

One-One-Six-One-One

Playing Orientation: Neutral (8-8)

No. of Strikers /Def players: (1/1)

Shape: Quadrilateral

Shape spread: (7X5)

No. of half-side players (Neut): 7{(3(4)}

No. of Outer players (Inner): 4 (6)

No. of Mid-fielders (Neut): 8(6)

No. of Att/Def Mid-fielders: (1/1)

One-Two-One-One-Five and Five-One-One-Two-One

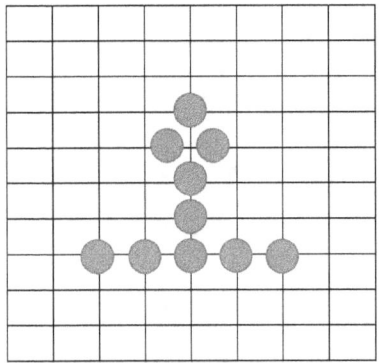

	One-Two-One-One-Five	Five-One-One-Two-One
Playing Orientation:	Defensive (7-4)	Attacking (4-7)
No. of Strikers /Def players:	(1/5)	(5/1)
Shape:	Triangle	
Shape spread:	(7X5)	
No. of half-side players (Neut):	7{(3(4)}	
No. of Outer players (Inner):	6 (4)	
No. of Mid-fielders (Neut):	4(1)	
No. of Att/Def Mid-fielders:	(2/1)	(1/2)

One-Two-One-Five-One and One-Five-One-Two-One

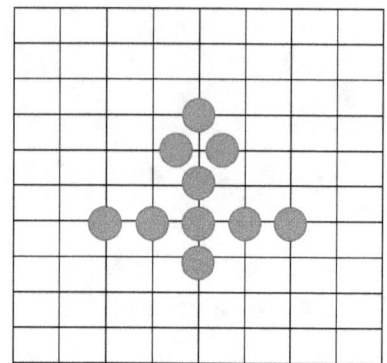

	One-Two-One-Five-One	One-Five-One-Two-One
Playing Orientation:	Defensive (7-4)	Attacking (4-7)
No. of Strikers /Def players:	(1/1)	(1/1)
Shape:	Quadrilateral	
Shape spread:	(7X5)	
No. of half-side players (Neut):	7{(3(4)}	
No. of Outer players (Inner):	4 (6)	
No. of Mid-fielders (Neut):	8(1)	
No. of Att/Def Mid-fielders:	(2/5)	(5/2)

One-Two-One-Two-Four and Four-Two-One-Two-One

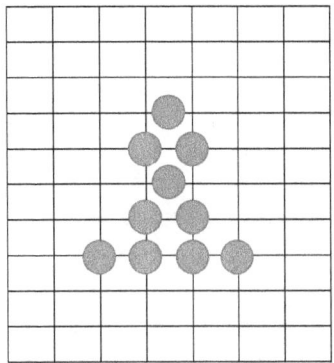

	One-Two-One-Two-Four	Four-Two-One-Two-One
Playing Orientation:	Defensive (7-4)	Attacking (4-7)
No. of Strikers /Def players:	(1/4)	(4/1)
Shape:	Pentagon	
Shape spread:	(5X5)	
No. of half-side players (Neut):	6{(4(2)}	
No. of Outer players (Inner):	7 (3)	
No. of Mid-fielders (Neut):	5(1)	
No. of Att/Def Mid-fielders:	(2/2)	(2/2)

One-Two-One-Three-Three and Three-Three-One-Two-One

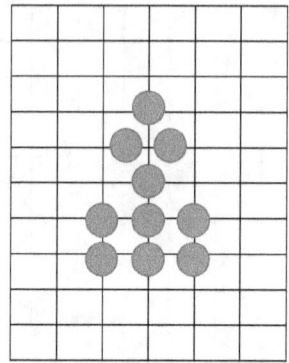

	One-Two-One-Three-Three	Three-Three-One-Two-One
Playing Orientation:	Defensive (7-4)	Attacking (4-7)
No. of Strikers /Def players:	(1/3)	(3/1)
Shape:	Heptagon	
Shape spread:	(5X5)	
No. of half-side players (Neut):	7{(3(4)}	
No. of Outer players (Inner):	8 (2)	
No. of Mid-fielders (Neut):	6(1)	
No. of Att/Def Mid-fielders:	(2/3)	(3/2)

One-Two-One-Four-Two and Two-Four-One-Two-One

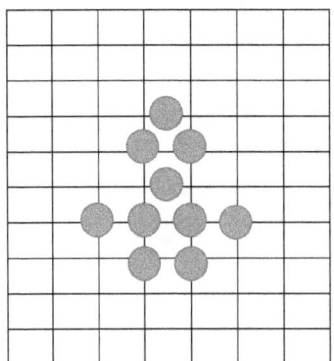

	One-Two-One-Four-Two	Two-Four-One-Two-One
Playing Orientation:	Defensive (7-4)	Attacking (4-7)
No. of Strikers /Def players:	(1/2)	(2/1)
Shape:	Pentagon	
Shape spread:	(5X5)	
No. of half-side players (Neut):	6{(4(2)}	
No. of Outer players (Inner):	7 (3)	
No. of Mid-fielders (Neut):	7(1)	
No. of Att/Def Mid-fielders:	(2/4)	(4/2)

One-Two-Two-One-Four and Four-One-Two-Two-One

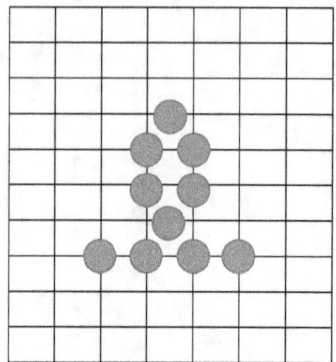

	One-Two-Two-One-Four	Four-One-Two-Two-One
Playing Orientation:	Defensive (7-5)	Attacking (5-7)
No. of Strikers /Def players:	(1/4)	(4/1)
Shape:	Pentagon	
Shape spread:	(5X5)	
No. of half-side players (Neut):	6{(4(2)}	
No. of Outer players (Inner):	7 (3)	
No. of Mid-fielders (Neut):	5(2)	
No. of Att/Def Mid-fielders:	(2/1)	(1/2)

One-Two-Two-Two-Three and Three-Two-Two-Two-One

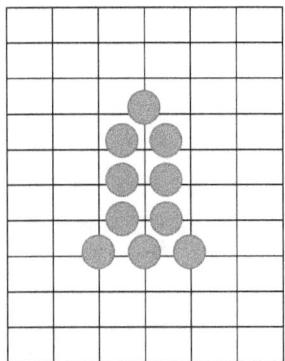

	One-Two-Two-Two-Three	Three-Two-Two-Two-One
Playing Orientation:	Defensive (7-5)	Attacking (5-7)
No. of Strikers /Def players:	(1/3)	(3/1)
Shape:	Pentagon	
Shape spread:	(5X5)	
No. of half-side players (Neut):	6{(4(2)}	
No. of Outer players (Inner):	6 (4)	
No. of Mid-fielders (Neut):	6(2)	
No. of Att/Def Mid-fielders:	(2/2)	(2/2)

One-Two-Two-Three-Two and Two-Three-Two-Two-One

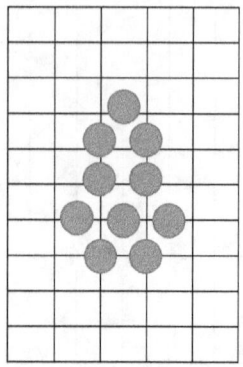

	One-Two-Two-Three-Two	Two-Three-Two-Two-One
Playing Orientation:	Defensive (7-5)	Attacking (5-7)
No. of Strikers /Def players:	(1/2)	(2/1)
Shape:	Heptagon	
Shape spread:	(5X5)	
No. of half-side players (Neut):	6{(4(2)}	
No. of Outer players (Inner):	7 (3)	
No. of Mid-fielders (Neut):	7(2)	
No. of Att/Def Mid-fielders:	(2/3)	(3/2)

One-Two-Two-Four-One and One-Four-Two-Two-One

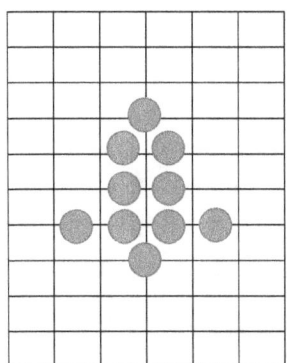

	One-Two-Two-Four-One	One-Four-Two-Two-One
Playing Orientation:	Defensive (7-5)	Attacking (5-7)
No. of Strikers /Def players:	(1/1)	(1/1)
Shape:	Quadrilateral	
Shape spread:	(5X5)	
No. of half-side players (Neut):	6{(4(2)}	
No. of Outer players (Inner):	6 (4)	
No. of Mid-fielders (Neut):	8(2)	
No. of Att/Def Mid-fielders:	(2/4)	(4/2)

One-Two-Three-One-Three and Three-One-Three-Two-One

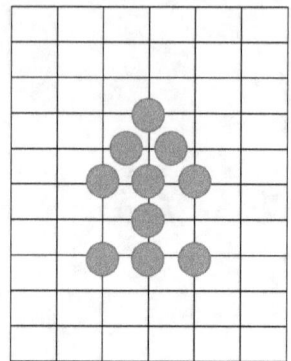

	One-Two-Three-One-Three	Three-One-Three-Two-One
Playing Orientation:	Defensive (7-6)	Attacking (6-7)
No. of Strikers /Def players:	(1/3)	(3/1)
Shape:	Pentagon	
Shape spread:	(5X5)	
No. of half-side players (Neut):	7{(3(4)}	
No. of Outer players (Inner):	8 (2)	
No. of Mid-fielders (Neut):	6(3)	
No. of Att/Def Mid-fielders:	(2/1)	(1/2)

One-Two-Three-Two-Two and Two-Two-Three-Two-One

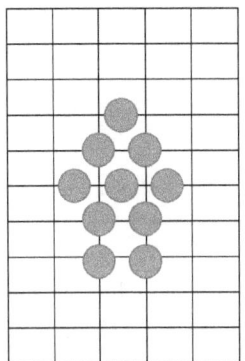

	One-Two-Three-Two-Two	Two-Two-Three-Two-One
Playing Orientation:	Defensive (7-6)	Attacking (6-7)
No. of Strikers /Def players:	(1/2)	(2/1)
Shape:	Pentagon	
Shape spread:	(5X5)	
No. of half-side players (Neut):	6{(4(2)}	
No. of Outer players (Inner):	7 (3)	
No. of Mid-fielders (Neut):	7(3)	
No. of Att/Def Mid-fielders:	(2/2)	(2/2)

One-Two-Three-Three-One and One-Three-Three-Two-One

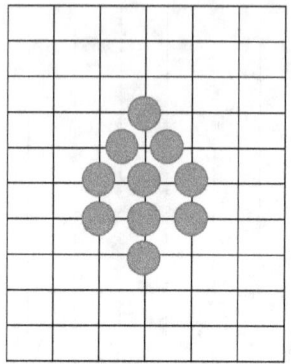

	One-Two-Three-Three-One	One-Three-Three-Two-One
Playing Orientation:	Defensive (7-6)	Attacking (6-7)
No. of Strikers /Def players:	(1/1)	(1/1)
Shape:	Hexagon	
Shape spread:	(5X5)	
No. of half-side players (Neut):	7{(3(4)}	
No. of Outer players (Inner):	8 (2)	
No. of Mid-fielders (Neut):	8(3)	
No. of Att/Def Mid-fielders:	(2/3)	(3/2)

One-Two-Four-One-Two and Two-One-Four-Two-One

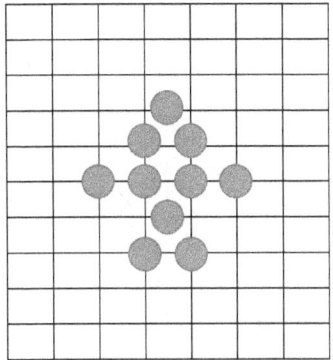

	One-Two-Four-One-Two	Two-One-Four-Two-One
Playing Orientation:	Neutral (7-7)	
No. of Strikers /Def players:	(1/2)	(2/1)
Shape:	Pentagon	
Shape spread:	(5X5)	
No. of half-side players (Neut):	6{(4(2)}	
No. of Outer players (Inner):	5 (5)	
No. of Mid-fielders (Neut):	7(4)	
No. of Att/Def Mid-fielders:	(2/1)	(1/2)

One-Two-Four-Two-One

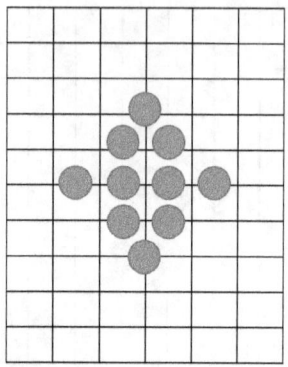

	One-Two-Four-Two-One
Playing Orientation:	Neutral (7-7)
No. of Strikers /Def players:	(1/1)
Shape:	Quadrilateral
Shape spread:	(5X5)
No. of half-side players (Neut):	6{(4(2)}
No. of Outer players (Inner):	4 (6)
No. of Mid-fielders (Neut):	8(4)
No. of Att/Def Mid-fielders:	(2/2)

One-Three-One-One-Four and Four-One-One-Three-One

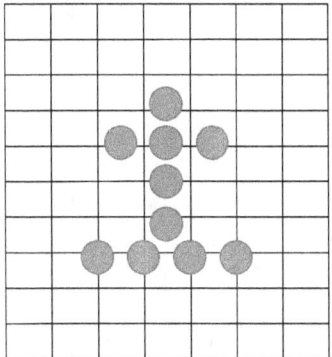

	One-Three-One-One-Four	Four-One-One-Three-One
Playing Orientation:	Defensive (6-5)	Attacking (5-6)
No. of Strikers /Def players:	(1/4)	(4/1)
Shape:	Pentagon	
Shape spread:	(7X5)	
No. of half-side players (Neut):	7{(3(4)}	
No. of Outer players (Inner):	7 (3)	
No. of Mid-fielders (Neut):	5(1)	
No. of Att/Def Mid-fielders:	(3/1)	(1/3)

One-Three-One-Two-Three and Three-Two-One-Three-One

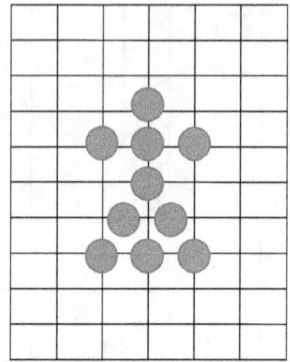

	One-Three-One-Two-Three	Three-Two-One-Three-One
Playing Orientation:	Defensive (6-5)	Attacking (5-6)
No. of Strikers /Def players:	(1/3)	(3/1)
Shape:	Pentagon	
Shape spread:	(5X5)	
No. of half-side players (Neut):	7{(3(4)}	
No. of Outer players (Inner):	6 (4)	
No. of Mid-fielders (Neut):	6(1)	
No. of Att/Def Mid-fielders:	(3/2)	(2/3)

One-Three-One-Three-Two and Two-Three-One-Three-One

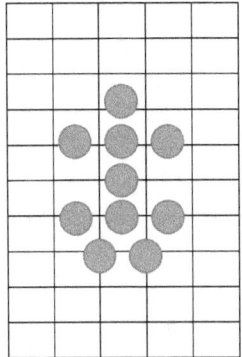

	One-Three-One-Three-Two	Two-Three-One-Three-One
Playing Orientation:	Attacking (6-5)	Defensive (5-6)
No. of Strikers /Def players:	(1/2)	(2/1)
Shape:	Heptagon	
Shape spread:	(5X5)	
No. of half-side players (Neut):	7{(3(4)}	
No. of Outer players (Inner):	7 (3)	
No. of Mid-fielders (Neut):	7(1)	
No. of Att/Def Mid-fielders:	(3/3)	(3/3)

One-Three-One-Four-One and One-Four-One-Three-One

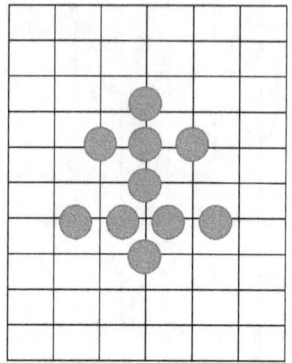

	One-Three-One-Four-One	One-Four-One-Three-One
Playing Orientation:	Defensive (6-5)	Attacking (5-6)
No. of Strikers /Def players:	(1/1)	(1/1)
Shape:	Hexagon	
Shape spread:	(7X5)	
No. of half-side players (Neut):	7{(3(4)}	
No. of Outer players (Inner):	6 (4)	
No. of Mid-fielders (Neut):	8(1)	
No. of Att/Def Mid-fielders:	(3/4)	(4/3)

One-Three-Two-One-Three and Three-One-Two-Three-One

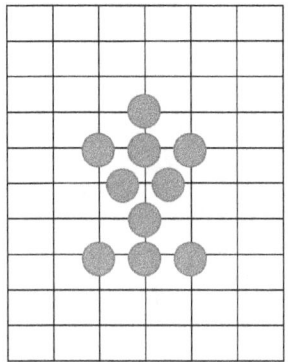

	One-Three-Two-One-Three	Three-One-Two-Three-One
Playing Orientation:	Neutral (6-6)	
No. of Strikers /Def players:	(1/3)	(3/1)
Shape:	Pentagon	
Shape spread:	(5X5)	
No. of half-side players (Neut):	7{(3(4)}	
No. of Outer players (Inner):	6 (4)	
No. of Mid-fielders (Neut):	6(2)	
No. of Att/Def Mid-fielders:	(3/1)	(1/3)

One-Three-Two-Three-One

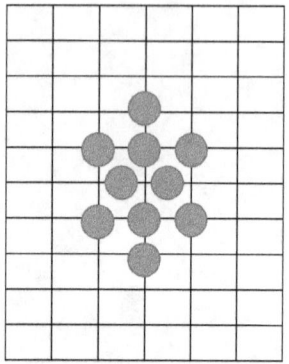

One-Three-Two-Three-One

Playing Orientation:	Neutral (6-6)
No. of Strikers /Def players:	(1/1)
Shape:	Hexagon
Shape spread:	(5X5)
No. of half-side players (Neut):	7{(3(4)}
No. of Outer players (Inner):	6 (4)
No. of Mid-fielders (Neut):	8(2)
No. of Att/Def Mid-fielders:	(3/3)

One-Three-Two-Two-Two and Two-Two-Two-Three-One

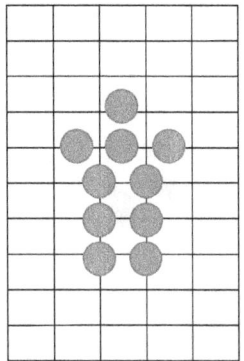

	One-Three-Two-Two-Two	Two-Two-Two-Three-One
Playing Orientation:	Neutral (6-6)	
No. of Strikers /Def players:	(1/2)	(2/1)
Shape:	Pentagon	
Shape spread:	(5X5)	
No. of half-side players (Neut):	6{(4(2)}	
No. of Outer players (Inner):	5 (5)	
No. of Mid-fielders (Neut):	7(2)	
No. of Att/Def Mid-fielders:	(3/2)	(2/3)

One-Three-Three-One-Two and Two-One-Three-Three-One

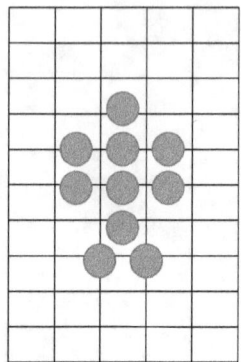

	One-Three-Three-One-Two	Two-One-Three-Three-One
Playing Orientation:	Attacking (6-7)	Defensive (7-6)
No. of Strikers /Def players:	(1/2)	(2/1)
Shape:	Heptagon	
Shape spread:	(5X5)	
No. of half-side players (Neut):	7{(3(4)}	
No. of Outer players (Inner):	7 (3)	
No. of Mid-fielders (Neut):	7(3)	
No. of Att/Def Mid-fielders:	(3/1)	(1/3)

One-Four-One-One-Three and Three-One-One-Four-One

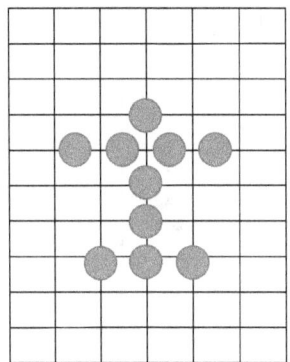

	One-Four-One-One-Three	Three-One-One-Four-One
Playing Orientation:	Attacking (5-6)	Defensive (6-5)
No. of Strikers /Def players:	(1/3)	(3/1)
Shape:	Pentagon	
Shape Orientation:	(7X5)	
No. of half-side players (Neut):	7{(3(4)}	
No. of Outer players (Inner):	6 (4)	
No. of Mid-fielders (Neut):	6(1)	
No. of Att/Def Mid-fielders:	(4/1)	(1/4)

One-Four-One-Two-Two and Two-Two-One-Four-One

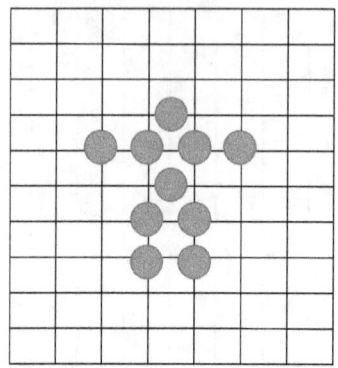

	One-Four-One-Two-Two	Two-Two-One-Four-One
Number of Inner players:	Attacking (5-6)	Defensive (6-5)
No. of Strikers /Def players:	(1/2)	(2/1)
Shape:	Pentagon	
Shape spread:	(5X5)	
No. of half-side players (Neut):	6{(4(2)}	
No. of Outer players (Inner):	5 (5)	
No. of Mid-fielders (Neut):	7(1)	
No. of Att/Def Mid-fielders:	(4/2)	(2/4)

One-Four-Two-One-Two and Two-One-Two-Four-One

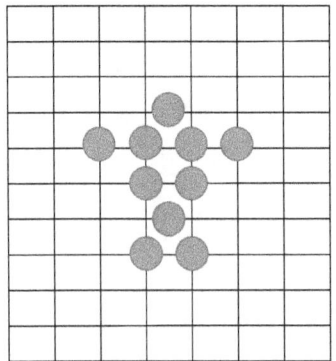

	One-Four-Two-One-Two	Two-One-Two-Four-One
Playing Orientation:	Attacking (5-7)	Defensive (7-5)
No. of Strikers /Def players:	(1/2)	(2/1)
Shape:	Pentagon	
Shape spread:	(5X5)	
No. of half-side players (Neut):	6{(4(2)}	
No. of Outer players (Inner):	5 (5)	
No. of Mid-fielders (Neut):	7(2)	
No. of Att/Def Mid-fielders:	(4/1)	(1/4)

One-Five-One-One-Two and Two-One-One-Five-One

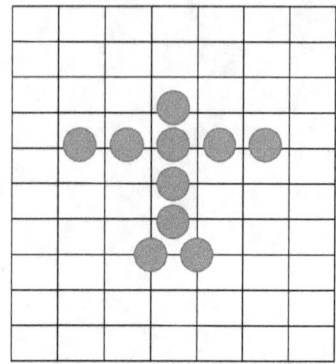

	One-Five-One-One-Two	Two-One-One-Five-One
Playing Orientation:	Attacking (4-7)	Defensive (7-4)
No. of Strikers /Def players:	(1/2)	(2/1)
Shape:	Pentagon	
Shape spread:	(7X5)	
No. of half-side players (Neut):	7{(3(4)}	
No. of Outer players (Inner):	5 (5)	
No. of Mid-fielders (Neut):	7(1)	
No. of Att/Def Mid-fielders:	(5/1)	(1/5)

Two-One-One-One-Five and Five-One-One-One-Two

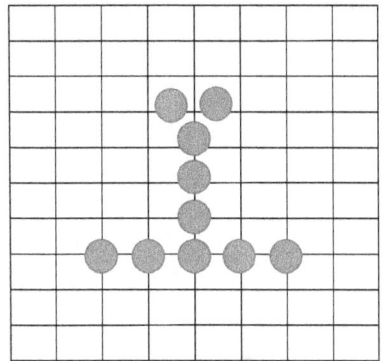

	Two-One-One-One-Five	Five-One-One-One-Two
Playing Orientation:	Defensive (7-4)	Attacking (4-7)
No. of Strikers /Def players:	(2/5)	(5/2)
Shape:	Trapezium	
Shape spread:	(7X5)	
No. of half-side players (Neut):	7{(3(4)}	
No. of Outer players (Inner):	7 (3)	
No. of Mid-fielders (Neut):	3(1)	
No. of Att/Def Mid-fielders:	(1/1)	(1/1)

Two-One-One-Two-Four and Four-Two-One-One-Two

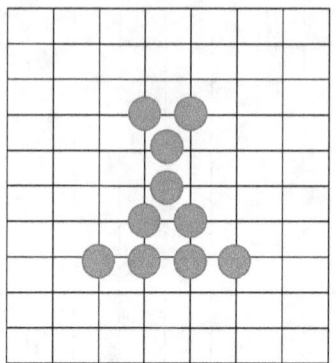

	Two-One-One-Two-Four	Four-Two-One-One-Two
Playing Orientation:	Defensive (7-4)	Attacking (4-7)
No. of Strikers /Def players:	(2/4)	(4/2)
Shape:	Trapezium	
Shape Orientation:	(5X5)	
No. of half-side players (Neut):	6{(4(2)}	
No. of Outer players (Inner):	6 (4)	
No. of Mid-fielders (Neut):	4(1)	
No. of Att/Def Mid-fielders:	(1/2)	(2/1)

Two-One-One-Three-Three and Three-Three-One-One-Two

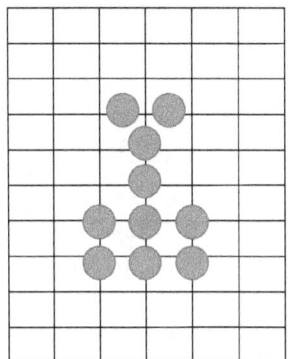

	Two-One-One-Three-Three	Three-Three-One-One-Two
Playing Orientation:	Defensive (7-4)	Attacking (4-7)
No. of Strikers /Def players:	(2/3)	(3/2)
Shape:	Hexagon	
Shape spread:	(5X5)	
No. of half-side players (Neut):	7{(3(4)}	
No. of Outer players (Inner):	7 (3)	
No. of Mid-fielders (Neut):	5(1)	
No. of Att/Def Mid-fielders:	(1/3)	(3/1)

Two-One-Two-One-Four and Four-One-Two-One-Two

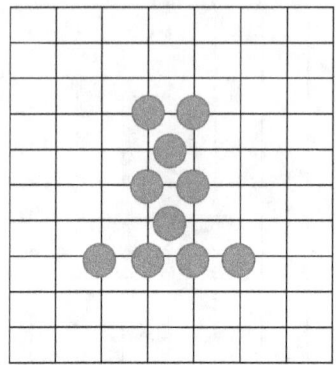

	Two-One-Two-One-Four	Four-One-Two-One-Two
Playing Orientation:	Defensive (7-5)	Attacking (5-7)
No. of Strikers /Def players:	(2/4)	(4/2)
Shape:	Trapezium	
Shape spread:	(5X5)	
No. of half-side players (Neut):	6{(4(2)}	
No. of Outer players (Inner):	6 (4)	
No. of Mid-fielders (Neut):	4(2)	
No. of Att/Def Mid-fielders:	(1/1)	(1/1)

Two-One-Two-Two-Three and Three-Two-Two-One-Two

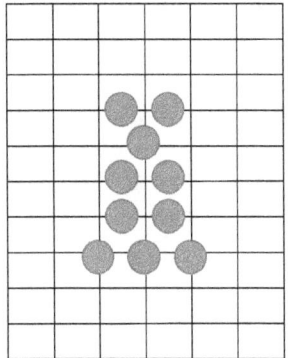

	Two-One-Two-Two-Three	Three-Two-Two-One-Two
Playing Orientation:	Defensive (7-5)	Attacking (5-7)
No. of Strikers /Def players:	(2/3)	(3/2)
Shape:	Trapezium	
Shape spread:	(5X5)	
No. of half-side players (Neut):	6{(4(2)}	
No. of Outer players (Inner):	5 (5)	
No. of Mid-fielders (Neut):	5(2)	
No. of Att/Def Mid-fielders:	(1/2)	(2/1)

Two-One-Three-One-Three and Three-One-Three-One-Two

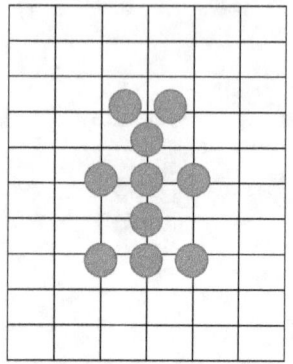

	Two-One-Three-One-Three	Three-One-Three-One-Two
Playing Orientation:	Defensive (7-6)	Attacking (6-7)
No. of Strikers /Def players:	(2/3)	(3/2)
Shape:	Hexagon	
Shape spread:	(5X5)	
No. of half-side players (Neut):	7{(3(4)}	
No. of Outer players (Inner):	7 (3)	
No. of Mid-fielders (Neut):	4(3)	
No. of Att/Def Mid-fielders:	(1/1)	(1/1)

Two-One-Three-Two-Two and Two-Two-Three-One-Two

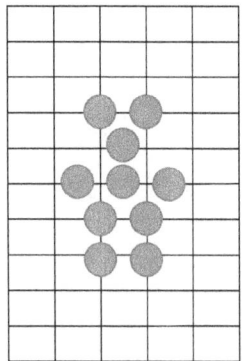

	Two-One-Three-Two-Two	Two-Two-Three-One-Two
Playing Orientation:	Defensive (7-6)	Attacking (6-7)
No. of Strikers /Def players:	(2/2)	(2/2)
Shape:	Hexagon	
Shape spread:	(5X5)	
No. of half-side players (Neut):	6{(4(2)}	
No. of Outer players (Inner):	6 (4)	
No. of Mid-fielders (Neut):	6(3)	
No. of Att/Def Mid-fielders:	(1/2)	(2/1)

Two-One-Four-One-Two

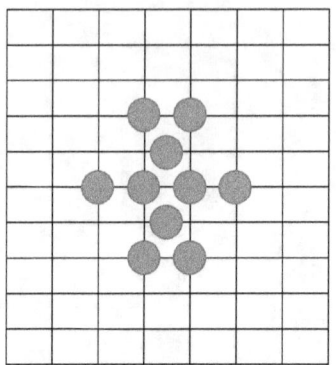

	Two-One-Four-One-Two
Playing Orientation:	Neutral (7-7)
No. of Strikers /Def players:	(2/2)
Shape:	Hexagon
Shape spread:	(5X5)
No. of half-side players (Neut):	6{(4(2)}
No. of Outer players (Inner):	6 (4)
No. of Mid-fielders (Neut):	6(4)
No. of Att/Def Mid-fielders:	(1/1)

Two-Two-One-One-Four and Four-One-One-Two-Two

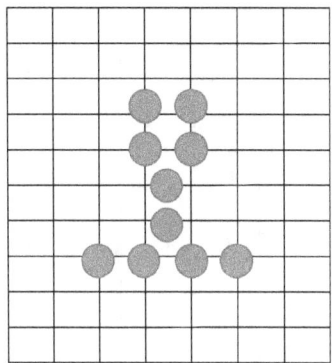

	Two-Two-One-One-Four	Four-One-One-Two-Two
Playing Orientation:	Defensive (6-5)	Attacking (5-6)
No. of Strikers /Def players:	(2/4)	(4/2)
Shape:	Trapezium	
Shape spread:	(5X5)	
No. of half-side players (Neut):	6{(4(2)}	
No. of Outer players (Inner):	6 (4)	
No. of Mid-fielders (Neut):	4(1)	
No. of Att/Def Mid-fielders:	(2/1)	(1/2)

Two-Two-One-Two-Three and Three-Two-One-Two-Two

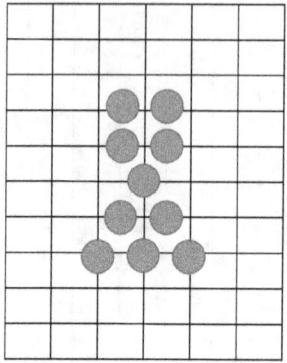

	Two-Two-One-Two-Three	Three-Two-One-Two-Two
Playing Orientation:	Defensive (6-5)	Attacking (5-6)
No. of Strikers /Def players:	(2/3)	(3/2)
Shape:	Trapezium	
Shape spread:	(5X5)	
No. of half-side players (Neut):	6{(4(2)}	
No. of Outer players (Inner):	5 (5)	
No. of Mid-fielders (Neut):	5(1)	
No. of Att/Def Mid-fielders:	(2/2)	(2/2)

Two-Two-Two-One-Three and Three-One-Two-Two-Two

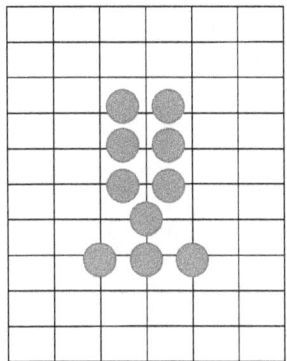

	Two-Two-Two-One-Three	Three-One-Two-Two-Two
Playing Orientation:	Neutral (6-6)	
No. of Strikers /Def players:	(2/3)	(3/2)
Shape:	Trapezium	
Shape spread:	(5X5)	
No. of half-side players (Neut):	6{(4(2)}	
No. of Outer players (Inner):	5 (5)	
No. of Mid-fielders (Neut):	5(2)	
No. of Att/Def Mid-fielders:	(2/1)	(1/2)

Two-Two-Two-Two-Two

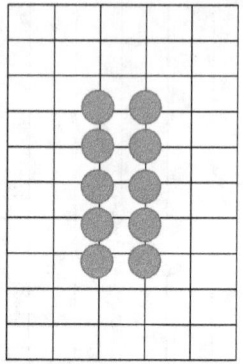

Two-Two-Two-Two-Two

Playing Orientation: Neutral (6-6)

No. of Strikers /Def players: (2/2)

Shape: Rectangle

Shape spread: (2X5)

No. of half-side players (Neut): 5{(5(0)}

No. of Outer players (Inner): 10 (0)

No. of Mid-fielders (Neut): 6(2)

No. of Att/Def Mid-fielders: (2/2)

Two-Three-One-One-Three and Three-One-One-Three-Two

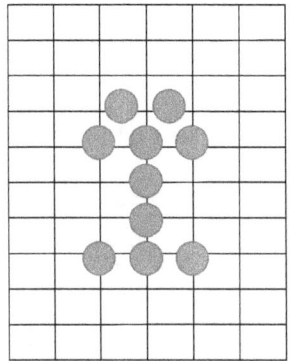

	Two-Three-One-One-Three	Three-One-One-Three-Two
Playing Orientation:	Attacking (5-6)	Defensive (6-5)
No. of Strikers /Def players:	(2/3)	(3/2)
Shape:	Hexagon	
Shape spread:	(5X5)	
No. of half-side players (Neut):	7{(3(4)}	
No. of Outer players (Inner):	7 (3)	
No. of Mid-fielders (Neut):	5(1)	
No. of Att/Def Mid-fielders:	(3/1)	(1/3)

Two-Three-One-Two-Two and Two-Two-One-Three-Two

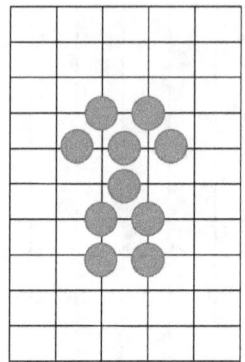

	Two-Three-One-Two-Two	Two-Two-One-Three-Two
Playing Orientation:	Attacking (5-6)	Defensive (6-5)
No. of Strikers /Def players:	(2/2)	(2/2)
Shape:	Hexagon	
Shape spread:	(5X5)	
No. of half-side players (Neut):	6{(4(2)}	
No. of Outer players (Inner):	6 (4)	
No. of Mid-fielders (Neut):	6(1)	
No. of Att/Def Mid-fielders:	(3/2)	(2/3)

Two-Three-Two-One-Two and Two-One-Two-Three-Two

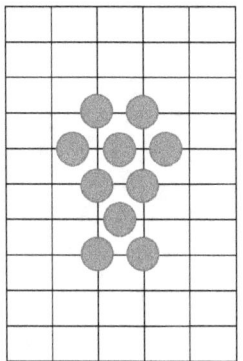

	Two-Three-Two-One-Two	Two-One-Two-Three-Two
Playing Orientation:	Attacking (5-7)	Defensive (7-5)
No. of Strikers /Def players:	(2/2)	(2/2)
Shape:	Hexagon	
Shape spread:	(5X5)	
No. of half-side players (Neut):	6{(4(2)}	
No. of Outer players (Inner):	6 (4)	
No. of Mid-fielders (Neut):	6(2)	
No. of Att/Def Mid-fielders:	(3/1)	(1/3)

Two-Four-One-One-Two and Two-One-One-Four-Two

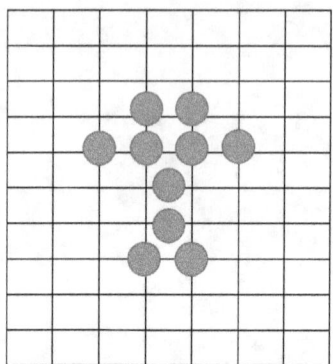

	Two-Four-One-One-Two	Two-One-One-Four-Two
Playing Orientation:	Attacking (4-7)	Defensive (7-4)
No. of Strikers /Def players:	(2/2)	(2/2)
Shape:	Hexagon	
Shape spread:	(5X5)	
No. of half-side players (Neut):	6{(4(2)}	
No. of Outer players (Inner):	6 (4)	
No. of Mid-fielders (Neut):	6(1)	
No. of Att/Def Mid-fielders:	(4/1)	(1/4)

Two-Four-Two-One-One and One-One-Two-Four-Two

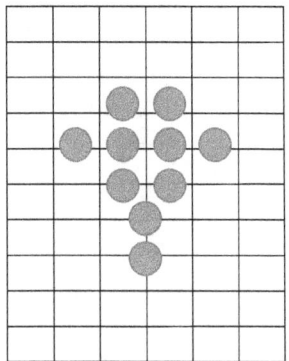

	Two-Four-Two-One-One	One-One-Two-Four-Two
Playing Orientation:	Attacking (4-8)	Defensive (8-4)
No. of Strikers /Def players:	(2/1)	(1/2)
Shape:	Pentagon	
Shape spread:	(5X5)	
No. of half-side players (Neut):	6{(4(2)}	
No. of Outer players (Inner):	5 (5)	
No. of Mid-fielders (Neut):	7(2)	
No. of Att/Def Mid-fielders:	(4/1)	(1/4)

Three-One-One-One-Four and Four-One-One-One-Three

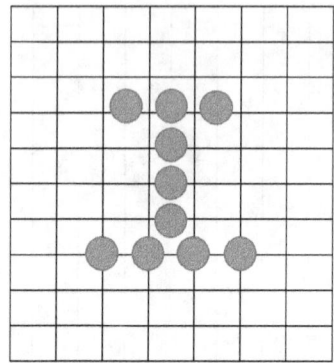

	Three-One-One-One-Four	Four-One-One-One-Three
Playing Orientation:	Defensive (6-5)	Attacking (5-6)
No. of Strikers /Def players:	(3/4)	(4/3)
Shape:	Trapezium	
Shape spread:	(7X5)	
No. of half-side players (Neut):	7{(3(4)}	
No. of Outer players (Inner):	7 (3)	
No. of Mid-fielders (Neut):	3(1)	
No. of Att/Def Mid-fielders:	(1/1)	(1/1)

Three-One-One-Two-Three and Three-Two-One-One-Three

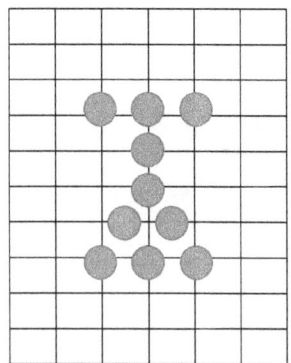

	Three-One-One-Two-Three	Three-Two-One-One-Three
Playing Orientation:	Defensive (6-5)	Attacking (5-6)
No. of Strikers /Def players:	(3/3)	(3/3)
Shape:	Rectangle	
Shape spread:	(5X5)	
No. of half-side players (Neut):	7{(3(4)}	
No. of Outer players (Inner):	6 (4)	
No. of Mid-fielders (Neut):	4(1)	
No. of Att/Def Mid-fielders:	(1/2)	(2/1)

Three-One-Two-One-Three

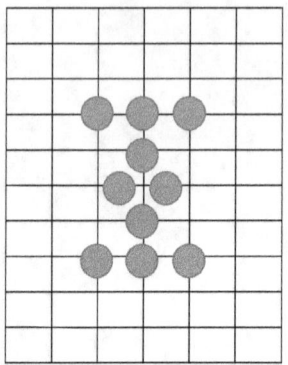

	Three-One-Two-One-Three
Playing Orientation:	Neutral (6-6)
No. of Strikers /Def players:	(3/3)
Shape:	Rectangle
Shape spread:	(5X5)
No. of half-side players (Neut):	7{(3(4)}
No. of Outer players (Inner):	6 (4)
No. of Mid-fielders (Neut):	4(2)
No. of Att/Def Mid-fielders:	(1/1)

LEVEL 6

Formations: 126

Symmetrically neutral: 6

One-One-One-One-One-Five and Five-One-One-One-One-One

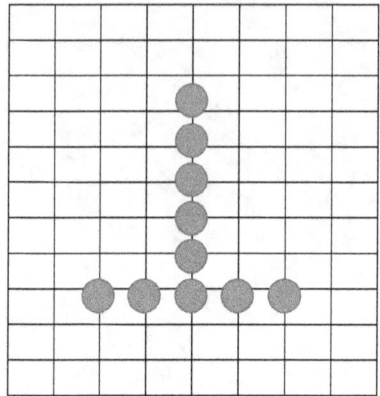

	One-One-One-One-One-Five	Five-One-One-One-One-One
Playing Orientation:	Defensive (7-3)	Attacking (3-7)
No. of Strikers /Def players:	(1/5)	(5/1)
Shape:	Triangle	
Shape spread:	(5X6)	
No. of half-side players (Neut):	8{(2(6)}	
No. of Outer players (Inner):	6 (4)	
No. of Mid-fielders (Neut):	4(0)	
No. of Att/Def Mid-fielders:	(2/2)	(2/2)

One-One-One-One-Two-Four and Four-Two-One-One-One-One

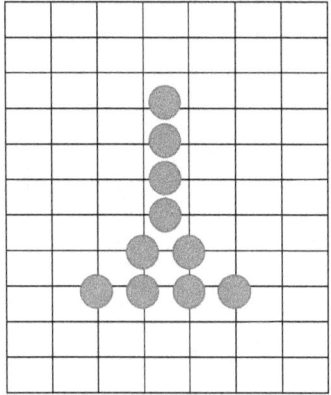

	One-One-One-One-Two-Four	Four-Two-One-One-One-One
Playing Orientation:	Defensive (7-3)	Attacking (3-7)
No. of Strikers /Def players:	(1/4)	(4/1)
Shape:	Triangle	
Shape spread:	(5X6)	
No. of half-side players (Neut):	7{(3(4)}	
No. of Outer players (Inner):	5 (5)	
No. of Mid-fielders (Neut):	5(0)	
No. of Att/Def Mid-fielders:	(2/3)	(3/2)

One-One-One-One-Three-Three and Three-Three-One-One-One-One

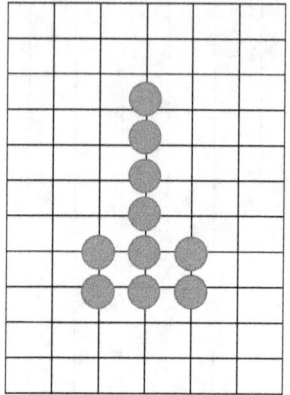

	One-One-One-One-Three-Three	Three-Three-One-One-One-One
Playing Orientation:	Defensive (7-3)	Attacking (3-7)
No. of Strikers /Def players:	(1/3)	(3/1)
Shape:	Pentagon	
Shape spread:	(3X6)	
No. of half-side players (Neut):	8{(2(6)}	
No. of Outer players (Inner):	6 (4)	
No. of Mid-fielders (Neut):	6(0)	
No. of Att/Def Mid-fielders:	(2/4)	(4/2)

One-One-One-One-Five-One and One-Five-One-One-One-One

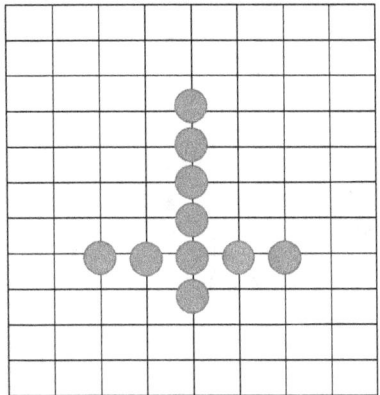

	One-One-One-One-Five-One	One-Five-One-One-One-One
Playing Orientation:	Defensive (7-3)	Attacking (3-7)
No. of Strikers /Def players:	(1/1)	(1/1)
Shape:	Quadrilateral	
Shape spread:	(5X6)	
No. of half-side players (Neut):	8{(2(6)}	
No. of Outer players (Inner):	4 (6)	
No. of Mid-fielders (Neut):	8(0)	
No. of Att/Def Mid-fielders:	(2/6)	(6/2)

One-One-One-Two-One-Four and Four-One-Two-One-One-One

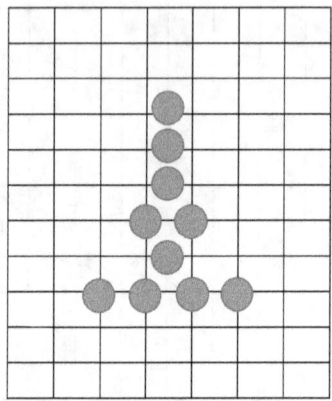

	One-One-One-Two-One-Four	Four-One-Two-One-One-One
Playing Orientation:	Defensive (7-3)	Attacking (3-7)
No. of Strikers /Def players:	(1/4)	(4/1)
Shape:	Triangle	
Shape spread:	(5X6)	
No. of half-side players (Neut):	7{(3(4)}	
No. of Outer players (Inner):	5 (5)	
No. of Mid-fielders (Neut):	5(0)	
No. of Att/Def Mid-fielders:	(2/3)	(3/2)

One-One-One-Two-Two-Three and Three-Two-Two-One-One-One

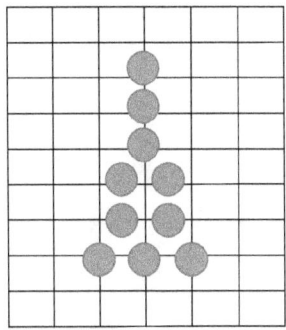

	One-One-One-Two-Two-Three	Three-Two-Two-One-One-One
Playing Orientation:	Defensive (7-3)	Attacking (3-7)
No. of Strikers /Def players:	(1/3)	(3/1)
Shape:	Triangle	
Shape spread:	(5X6)	
No. of half-side players (Neut):	7{(3(4)}	
No. of Outer players (Inner):	6 (4)	
No. of Mid-fielders (Neut):	6(0)	
No. of Att/Def Mid-fielders:	(2/4)	(4/2)

One-One-One-Three-One-Three and Three-One-Three-One-One-One

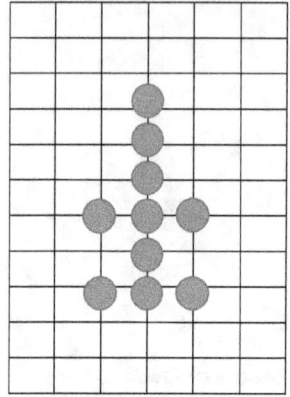

	One-One-One-Three-One-Three	Three-One-Three-One-One-One
Playing Orientation:	Defensive (7-3)	Attacking (3-7)
No. of Strikers /Def players:	(1/3)	(3/1)
Shape:	Pentagon	
Shape spread:	(3X6)	
No. of half-side players (Neut):	8{(2(6)}	
No. of Outer players (Inner):	6 (4)	
No. of Mid-fielders (Neut):	6(0)	
No. of Att/Def Mid-fielders:	(2/4)	(4/2)

One-One-One-Three-Two-Two and Two-Two-Three-One-One-One

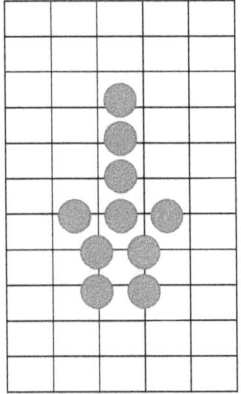

	One-One-One-Three-Two-Two	Two-Two-Three-One-One-One
Playing Orientation:	Defensive (7-3)	Attacking (3-7)
No. of Strikers /Def players:	(1/2)	(2/1)
Shape:	Pentagon	
Shape spread:	(5X6)	
No. of half-side players (Neut):	7{(3(4)}	
No. of Outer players (Inner):	5 (5)	
No. of Mid-fielders (Neut):	7(0)	
No. of Att/Def Mid-fielders:	(2/5)	(5/2)

One-One-One-Four-One-Two and Two-One-Four-One-One-One

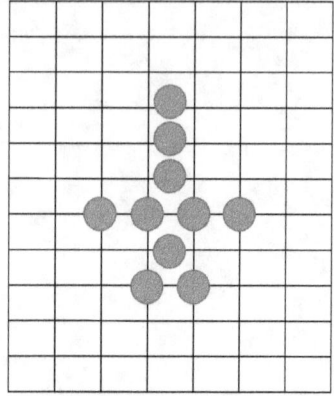

	One-One-One-Four-One-Two	Two-One-Four-One-One-One
Playing Orientation:	Defensive (7-3)	Attacking (3-7)
No. of Strikers /Def players:	(1/2)	(2/1)
Shape:	Pentagon	
Shape spread:	(5X6)	
No. of half-side players (Neut):	7{(3(4)}	
No. of Outer players (Inner):	5 (5)	
No. of Mid-fielders (Neut):	7(0)	
No. of Att/Def Mid-fielders:	(2/5)	(5/2)

One-One-One-Four-Two-One and One-Two-Four-One-One-One

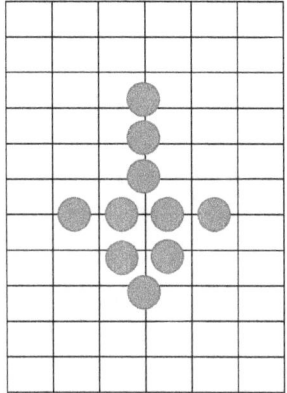

	One-One-One-Four-Two-One	One-Two-Four-One-One-One
Playing Orientation:	Defensive (7-3)	Attacking (3-7)
No. of Strikers /Def players:	(1/1)	(1/1)
Shape:	Quadrilateral	
Shape spread:	(5X6)	
No. of half-side players (Neut):	7{(3(4)}	
No. of Outer players (Inner):	4 (6)	
No. of Mid-fielders (Neut):	8(0)	
No. of Att/Def Mid-fielders:	(2/6)	(6/2)

One-One-One-Five-One-One and One-One-Five-One-One-One

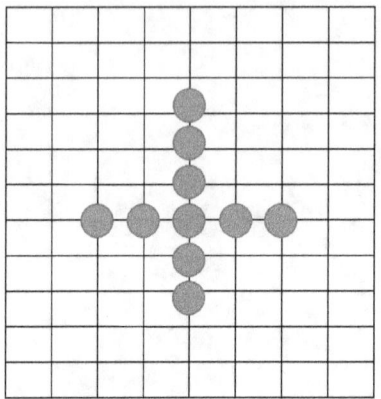

	One-One-One-Five-One-One	One-One-Five-One-One-One
Playing Orientation:	Defensive (7-3)	Attacking (3-7)
No. of Strikers /Def players:	(1/1)	(1/1)
Shape:	Quadrilateral	
Shape spread:	(5X6)	
No. of half-side players (Neut):	8{(2(6)}	
No. of Outer players (Inner):	4 (6)	
No. of Mid-fielders (Neut):	8(0)	
No. of Att/Def Mid-fielders:	(2/6)	(6/2)

One-One-Two-One-One-Four and Four-One-One-Two-One-One

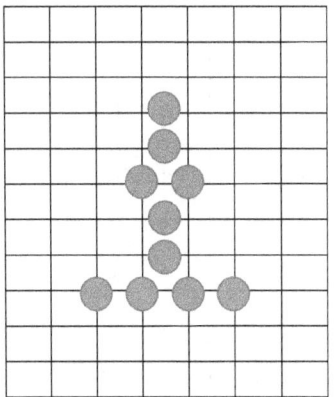

	One-One-Two-One-One-Four	Four-One-One-Two-One-One
Playing Orientation:	Defensive (6-4)	Attacking (4-6)
No. of Strikers /Def players:	(1/4)	(4/1)
Shape:	Triangle	
Shape spread:	(5X6)	
No. of half-side players (Neut):	7{(3(4)}	
No. of Outer players (Inner):	5 (5)	
No. of Mid-fielders (Neut):	5(0)	
No. of Att/Def Mid-fielders:	(3/2)	(2/3)

One-One-Two-One-Two-Three and Three-Two-One-Two-One-One

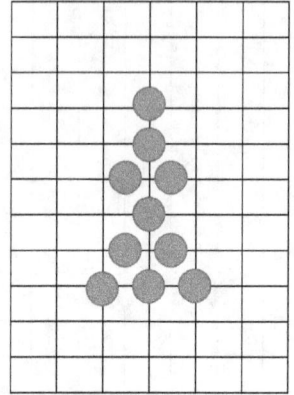

	One-One-Two-One-Two-Three	Three-Two-One-Two-One-One
Playing Orientation:	Defensive (6-4)	Attacking (4-6)
No. of Strikers /Def players:	(1/3)	(3/1)
Shape:	Pentagon	
Shape spread:	(5X6)	
No. of half-side players (Neut):	7{(3(4)}	
No. of Outer players (Inner):	6 (4)	
No. of Mid-fielders (Neut):	6(0)	
No. of Att/Def Mid-fielders:	(3/3)	(3/3)

One-One-Two-Two-One-Three and Three-One-Two-Two-One-One

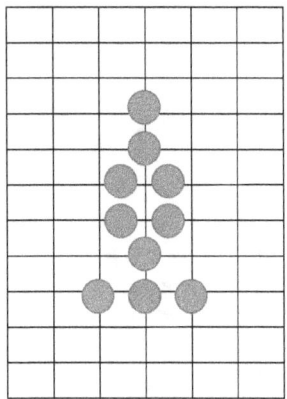

	One-One-Two-Two-One-Three	Three-One-Two-Two-One-One
Playing Orientation:	Defensive (6-4)	Attacking (4-6)
No. of Strikers /Def players:	(1/3)	(3/1)
Shape:	Pentagon	
Shape spread:	(5X6)	
No. of half-side players (Neut):	7{(3(4)}	
No. of Outer players (Inner):	6 (4)	
No. of Mid-fielders (Neut):	6(0)	
No. of Att/Def Mid-fielders:	(3/3)	(3/3)

One-One-Two-Two-Two-Two and Two-Two-Two-Two-One-One

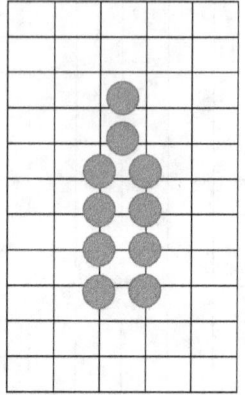

	One-One-Two-Two-Two-Two	Two-Two-Two-Two-One-One
Playing Orientation:	Defensive (6-4)	Attacking (4-6)
No. of Strikers /Def players:	(1/2)	(2/1)
Shape:	Pentagon	
Shape spread:	(3X6)	
No. of half-side players (Neut):	6{(4(2)}	
No. of Outer players (Inner):	9 (1)	
No. of Mid-fielders (Neut):	7(0)	
No. of Att/Def Mid-fielders:	(3/4)	(4/3)

One-One-Two-Three-One-Two and Two-One-Three-Two-One-One

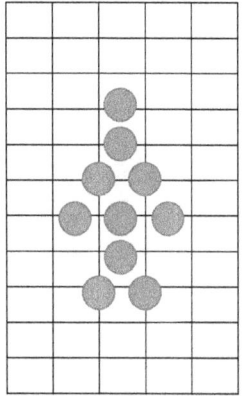

	One-One-Two-Three-One-Two	Two-One-Three-Two-One-One
Playing Orientation:	Defensive (6-4)	Attacking (4-6)
No. of Strikers /Def players:	(1/2)	(2/1)
Shape:	Pentagon	
Shape spread:	(5X6)	
No. of half-side players (Neut):	7{(3(4)}	
No. of Outer players (Inner):	5 (5)	
No. of Mid-fielders (Neut):	7(0)	
No. of Att/Def Mid-fielders:	(3/4)	(4/3)

One-One-Three-One-One-Three and Three-One-One-Three-One-One

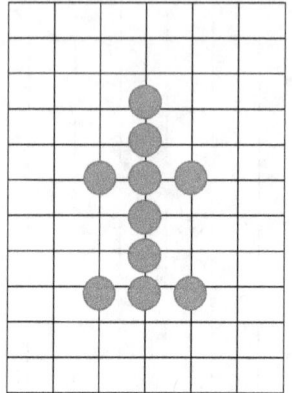

	One-One-Three-One-One-Three	Three-One-One-Three-One-One
Playing Orientation:	Neutral (5-5)	
No. of Strikers /Def players:	(1/3)	(3/1)
Shape:	Pentagon	
Shape spread:	(3X6)	
No. of half-side players (Neut):	8{(2(6)}	
No. of Outer players (Inner):	6 (4)	
No. of Mid-fielders (Neut):	6(0)	
No. of Att/Def Mid-fielders:	(4/2)	(2/4)

One-One-Three-One-Two-Two and Two-Two-One-Three-One-One

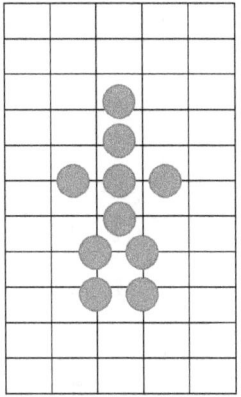

	One-One-Three-One-Two-Two	Two-Two-One-Three-One-One
Playing Orientation:	Neutral (5-5)	
No. of Strikers /Def players:	(1/2)	(2/1)
Shape:	Pentagon	
Shape spread:	(5X6)	
No. of half-side players (Neut):	7{(3(4)}	
No. of Outer players (Inner):	5 (5)	
No. of Mid-fielders (Neut):	7(0)	
No. of Att/Def Mid-fielders:	(4/3)	(3/4)

One-One-Three-One-Three-One and One-Three-One-Three-One-One

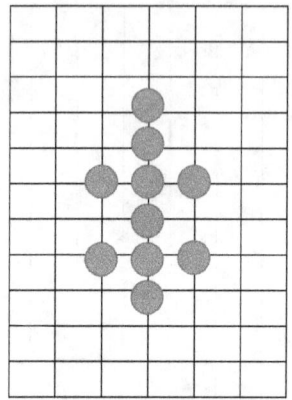

	One-One-Three-One-Three-One	One-Three-One-Three-One-One
Playing Orientation:	Neutral (5-5)	
No. of Strikers /Def players:	(1/1)	(1/1)
Shape:	Hexagon	
Shape spread:	(3X6)	
No. of half-side players (Neut):	8{(2(6)}	
No. of Outer players (Inner):	6 (4)	
No. of Mid-fielders (Neut):	8(0)	
No. of Att/Def Mid-fielders:	(4/4)	(4/4)

One-One-Three-Two-One-Two and Two-One-Two-Three-One-One

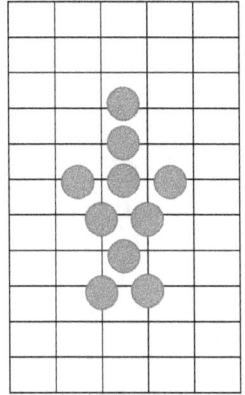

	One-One-Three-Two-One-Two	Two-One-Two-Three-One-One
Playing Orientation:	Neutral (5-5)	
No. of Strikers /Def players:	(1/2)	(2/1)
Shape:	Pentagon	
Shape spread:	(5X6)	
No. of half-side players (Neut):	7{(3(4)}	
No. of Outer players (Inner):	5 (5)	
No. of Mid-fielders (Neut):	7(0)	
No. of Att/Def Mid-fielders:	(4/3)	(3/4)

One-One-Three-Three-One-One

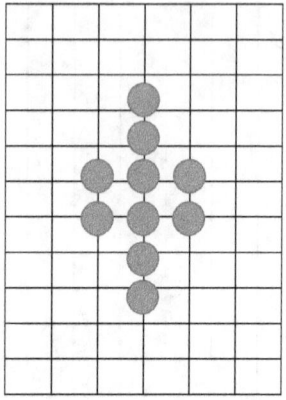

	One-One-Three-Three-One-One
Playing Orientation:	Neutral (5-5)
No. of Strikers /Def players:	(1/1)
Shape:	Hexagon
Shape spread:	(3X6)
No. of half-side players (Neut):	8{(2(6)}
No. of Outer players (Inner):	6 (4)
No. of Mid-fielders (Neut):	8(0)
No. of Att/Def Mid-fielders:	(4/4)

One-One-Four-One-One-Two and Two-One-One-Four-One-One

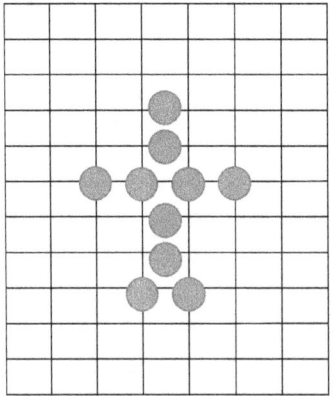

	One-One-Four-One-One-Two	Two-One-One-Four-One-One
Playing Orientation:	Attacking (4-6)	Defensive (6-4)
No. of Strikers /Def players:	(1/2)	(2/1)
Shape:	Pentagon	
Shape spread:	(5X6)	
No. of half-side players (Neut):	7{(3(4)}	
No. of Outer players (Inner):	5 (5)	
No. of Mid-fielders (Neut):	7(0)	
No. of Att/Def Mid-fielders:	(5/2)	(2/5)

One-One-Four-One-Two-One and One-Two-One-Four-One-One

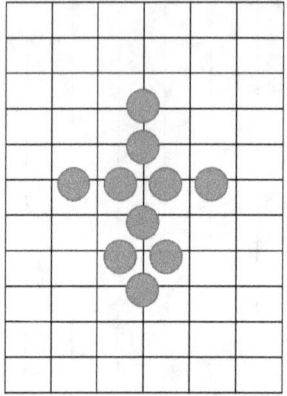

	One-One-Four-One-Two-One	One-Two-One-Four-One-One
Playing Orientation:	Attacking (4-6)	Defensive (6-4)
No. of Strikers /Def players:	(1/1)	(1/1)
Shape:	Quadrilateral	
Shape spread:	(5X6)	
No. of half-side players (Neut):	7{(3(4)}	
No. of Outer players (Inner):	6 (4)	
No. of Mid-fielders (Neut):	8(0)	
No. of Att/Def Mid-fielders:	(5/3)	(3/5)

One-One-Four-Two-One-One and One-One-Two-Four-One-One

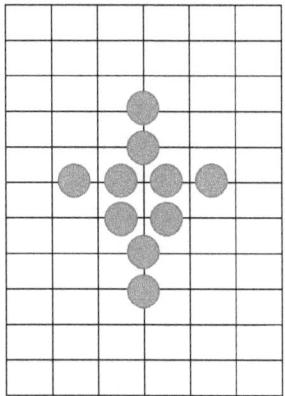

	One-One-Four-Two-One-One	One-One-Two-Four-One-One
Playing Orientation:	Attacking (4-6)	Defensive (6-4)
No. of Strikers /Def players:	(1/1)	(1/1)
Shape:	Quadrilateral	
Shape spread:	(5X6)	
No. of half-side players (Neut):	7{(3(4)}	
No. of Outer players (Inner):	4 (6)	
No. of Mid-fielders (Neut):	8(0)	
No. of Att/Def Mid-fielders:	(5/3)	(3/5)

One-Two-One-One-One-Four and Four-One-One-One-Two-One

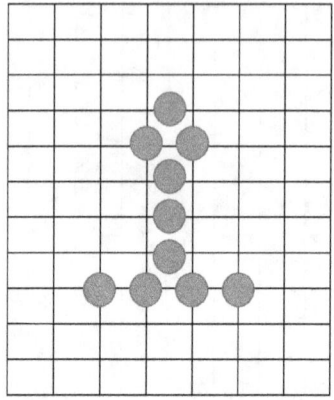

	One-Two-One-One-One-Four	Four-One-One-One-Two-One
Playing Orientation:	Defensive (6-4)	Attacking (4-6)
No. of Strikers /Def players:	(1/4)	(4/1)
Shape:	Pentagon	
Shape spread:	(5X6)	
No. of half-side players (Neut):	7{(3(4)}	
No. of Outer players (Inner):	7 (3)	
No. of Mid-fielders (Neut):	5(0)	
No. of Att/Def Mid-fielders:	(3/2)	(2/3)

One-Two-One-One-Two-Three and Three-Two-One-One-Two-One

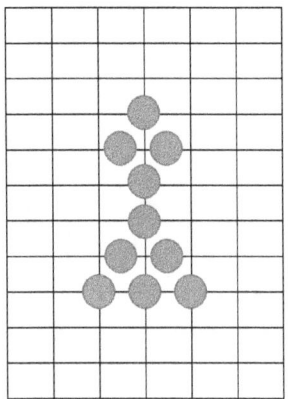

	One-Two-One-One-Two-Three	Three-Two-One-One-Two-One
Playing Orientation:	Defensive (6-4)	Attacking (4-6)
No. of Strikers /Def players:	(1/3)	(3/1)
Shape:	Pentagon	
Shape spread:	(5X6)	
No. of half-side players (Neut):	7{(3(4)}	
No. of Outer players (Inner):	6 (4)	
No. of Mid-fielders (Neut):	6(0)	
No. of Att/Def Mid-fielders:	(3/3)	(3/3)

One-Two-One-One-Three-Two and Two-Three-One-One-Two-One

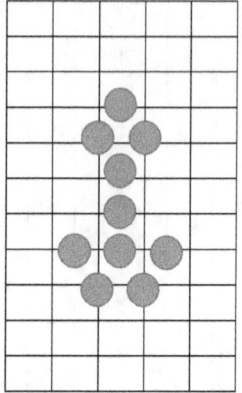

	One-Two-One-One-Three-Two	Two-Three-One-One-Two-One
Playing Orientation:	Defensive (6-4)	Attacking (4-6)
No. of Strikers /Def players:	(1/2)	(2/1)
Shape:	Heptagon	
Shape spread:	(5X6)	
No. of half-side players (Neut):	7{(3(4)}	
No. of Outer players (Inner):	7 (3)	
No. of Mid-fielders (Neut):	7(0)	
No. of Att/Def Mid-fielders:	(3/4)	(4/3)

One-Two-One-One-Four-One and One-Four-One-One-Two-One

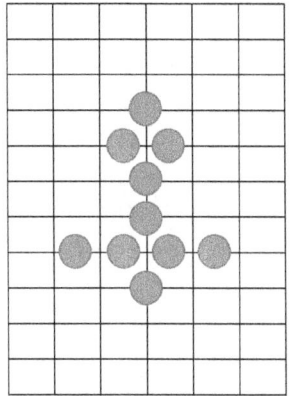

	One-Two-One-One-Four-One	One-Four-One-One-Two-One
Playing Orientation:	Defensive (6-4)	Attacking (4-6)
No. of Strikers /Def players:	(1/1)	(1/1)
Shape:	Quadrilateral	
Shape spread:	(5X6)	
No. of half-side players (Neut):	7{(3(4)}	
No. of Outer players (Inner):	6 (4)	
No. of Mid-fielders (Neut):	8(0)	
No. of Att/Def Mid-fielders:	(3/5)	(5/3)

One-Two-One-Two-One-Three and Three-One-Two-One-Two-One

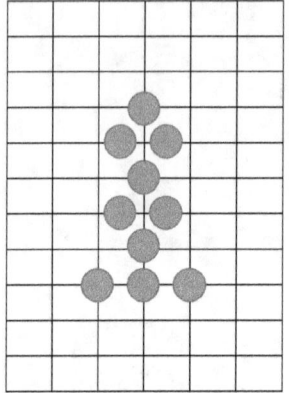

	One-Two-One-Two-One-Three	Three-One-Two-One-Two-One
Playing Orientation:	Defensive (6-4)	Attacking (4-6)
No. of Strikers /Def players:	(1/3)	(3/1)
Shape:	Pentagon	
Shape spread:	(5X6)	
No. of half-side players (Neut):	7{(3(4)}	
No. of Outer players (Inner):	6 (4)	
No. of Mid-fielders (Neut):	6(0)	
No. of Att/Def Mid-fielders:	(3/3)	(3/3)

One-Two-One-Two-Two-Two and Two-Two-Two-One-Two-One

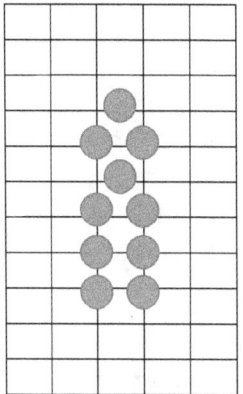

	One-Two-One-Two-Two-Two	Two-Two-Two-One-Two-One
Playing Orientation:	Defensive (6-4)	Attacking (4-6)
No. of Strikers /Def players:	(1/2)	(2/1)
Shape:	Pentagon	
Shape spread:	(3X6)	
No. of half-side players (Neut):	6{(4(2)}	
No. of Outer players (Inner):	9 (1)	
No. of Mid-fielders (Neut):	7(0)	
No. of Att/Def Mid-fielders:	(3/4)	(4/3)

One-Two-One-Two-Three-One and One-Three-Two-One-Two-One

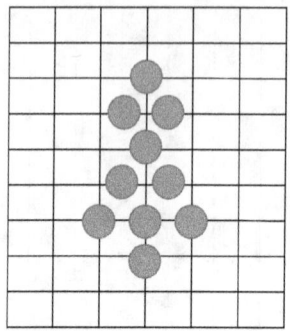

	One-Two-One-Two-Three-One	One-Three-Two-One-Two-One
Playing Orientation:	Defensive (6-4)	Attacking (4-6)
No. of Strikers /Def players:	(1/1)	(1/1)
Shape:	Hexagon	
Shape spread:	(5X6)	
No. of half-side players (Neut):	7{(3(4)}	
No. of Outer players (Inner):	6 (4)	
No. of Mid-fielders (Neut):	8(0)	
No. of Att/Def Mid-fielders:	(3/5)	(5/3)

One-Two-One-Three-One-Two and Two-One-Three-One-Two-One

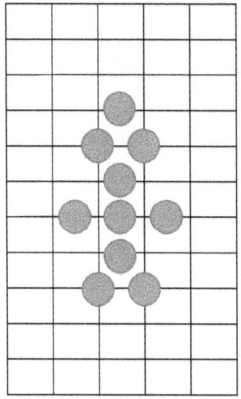

	One-Two-One-Three-One-Two	Two-One-Three-One-Two-One
Playing Orientation:	Defensive (6-4)	Attacking (4-6)
No. of Strikers /Def players:	(1/2)	(2/1)
Shape:	Heptagon	
Shape spread:	(5X6)	
No. of half-side players (Neut):	7{(3(4)}	
No. of Outer players (Inner):	7 (3)	
No. of Mid-fielders (Neut):	7(0)	
No. of Att/Def Mid-fielders:	(3/4)	(4/3)

One-Two-One-Three-Two-One and One-Two-Three-One-Two-One

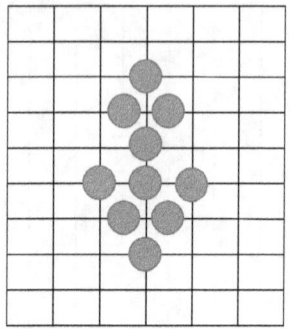

	One-Two-One-Three-Two-One	One-Two-Three-One-Two-One
Playing Orientation:	Defensive (6-4)	Attacking (4-6)
No. of Strikers /Def players:	(1/1)	(1/1)
Shape:	Hexagon	
Shape spread:	(5X6)	
No. of half-side players (Neut):	7{(3(4)}	
No. of Outer players (Inner):	8 (2)	
No. of Mid-fielders (Neut):	8(0)	
No. of Att/Def Mid-fielders:	(3/5)	(5/3)

One-Two-Two-One-One-Three and Three-One-One-Two-Two-One

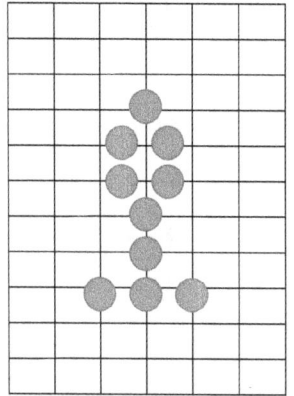

	One-Two-Two-One-One-Three	Three-One-One-Two-Two-One
Playing Orientation:	Neutral (5-5)	
No. of Strikers /Def players:	(1/3)	(3/1)
Shape:	Pentagon	
Shape spread:	(5X6)	
No. of half-side players (Neut):	7{(3(4)}	
No. of Outer players (Inner):	6 (4)	
No. of Mid-fielders (Neut):	6(0)	
No. of Att/Def Mid-fielders:	(4/2)	(2/4)

One-Two-Two-One-Two-Two and Two-Two-One-Two-Two-One

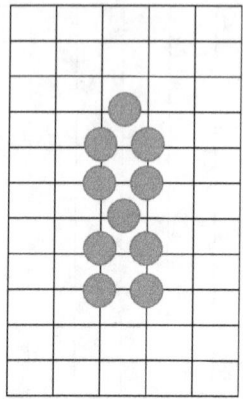

	One-Two-Two-One-Two-Two	Two-Two-One-Two-Two-One
Playing Orientation:	Neutral (5-5)	
No. of Strikers /Def players:	(1/2)	(2/1)
Shape:	Pentagon	
Shape spread:	(3X6)	
No. of half-side players (Neut):	6{(4(2)}	
No. of Outer players (Inner):	9 (1)	
No. of Mid-fielders (Neut):	7(0)	
No. of Att/Def Mid-fielders:	(4/3)	(3/4)

One-Two-Two-One-Three-One and One-Three-One-Two-Two-One

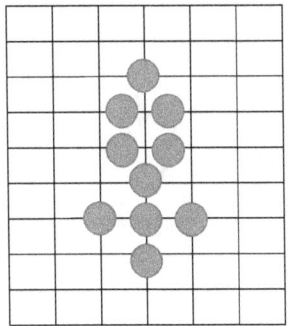

	One-Two-Two-One-Three-One	One-Three-One-Two-Two-One
Playing Orientation:	Neutral (5-5)	
No. of Strikers /Def players:	(1/1)	(1/1)
Shape:	Hexagon	
Shape spread:	(5X6)	
No. of half-side players (Neut):	7{(3(4)}	
No. of Outer players (Inner):	6 (4)	
No. of Mid-fielders (Neut):	8(0)	
No. of Att/Def Mid-fielders:	(4/4)	(4/4)

One-Two-Two-Two-One-Two and Two-One-Two-Two-Two-One

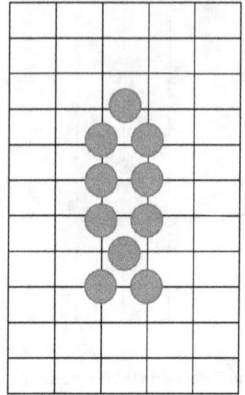

	One-Two-Two-Two-One-Two	Two-One-Two-Two-Two-One
Playing Orientation:	Neutral (5-5)	
No. of Strikers /Def players:	(1/2)	(2/1)
Shape:	Pentagon	
Shape spread:	(3X6)	
No. of half-side players (Neut):	6{(4(2)}	
No. of Outer players (Inner):	9 (1)	
No. of Mid-fielders (Neut):	7(0)	
No. of Att/Def Mid-fielders:	(4/3)	(3/4)

One-Two-Two-Two-Two-One

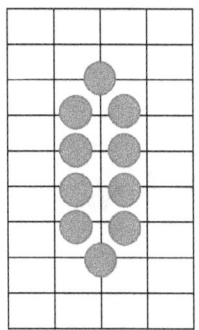

One-Two-Two-Two-Two-One

Playing Orientation:	Neutral (5-5)
No. of Strikers /Def players:	(1/1)
Shape:	Hexagon
Shape spread:	(3X6)
No. of half-side players (Neut):	6{(4(2)}
No. of Outer players (Inner):	10 (0)
No. of Mid-fielders (Neut):	8(0)
No. of Att/Def Mid-fielders:	(4/4)

One-Two-Two-Three-One-One and One-One-Three-Two-Two-One

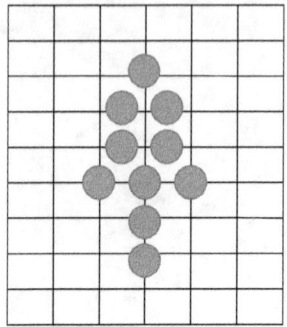

	One-Two-Two-Three-One-One	One-One-Three-Two-Two-One
Playing Orientation:	Neutral (5-5)	
No. of Strikers /Def players:	(1/1)	(1/1)
Shape:	Hexagon	
Shape spread:	(5X6)	
No. of half-side players (Neut):	7{(3(4)}	
No. of Outer players (Inner):	6 (4)	
No. of Mid-fielders (Neut):	8(0)	
No. of Att/Def Mid-fielders:	(4/4)	(4/4)

One-Two-Three-One-One-Two and Two-One-One-Three-Two-One

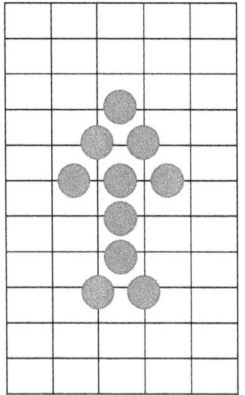

	One-Two-Three-One-One-Two	Two-One-One-Three-Two-One
Playing Orientation:	Attacking (4-6)	Defensive (6-4)
No. of Strikers /Def players:	(1/2)	(2/1)
Shape:	Pentagon	
Shape spread:	(5X6)	
No. of half-side players (Neut):	6{(3(4)}	
No. of Outer players (Inner):	7 (3)	
No. of Mid-fielders (Neut):	7(0)	
No. of Att/Def Mid-fielders:	(5/2)	(2/5)

One-Two-Three-Two-One-One and One-One-Two-Three-Two-One

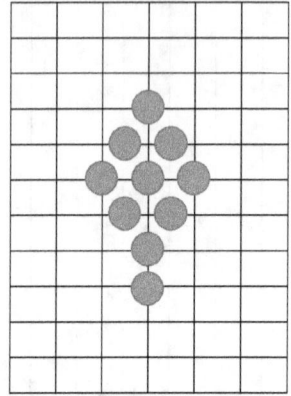

	One-Two-Three-Two-One-One	One-One-Two-Three-Two-One
Playing Orientation:	Attacking (4-6)	Defensive (6-4)
No. of Strikers /Def players:	(1/1)	(1/1)
Shape:	Quadrilateral	
Shape spread:	(5X6)	
No. of half-side players (Neut):	7{(3(4)}	
No. of Outer players (Inner):	6 (4)	
No. of Mid-fielders (Neut):	8(0)	
No. of Att/Def Mid-fielders:	(5/3)	(3/5)

One-Three-One-One-One-Three and Three-One-One-One-Three-One

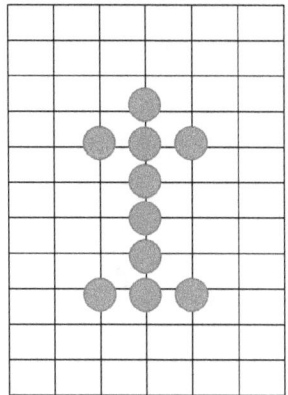

	One-Three-One-One-One-Three	Three-One-One-One-Three-One
Playing Orientation:	Neutral (5-5)	
No. of Strikers /Def players:	(1/3)	(3/1)
Shape:	Pentagon	
Shape spread:	(3X6)	
No. of half-side players (Neut):	8{(2(6)}	
No. of Outer players (Inner):	6 (4)	
No. of Mid-fielders (Neut):	6(0)	
No. of Att/Def Mid-fielders:	(4/2)	(2/4)

One-Three-One-One-Two-Two and Two-Two-One-One-Three-One

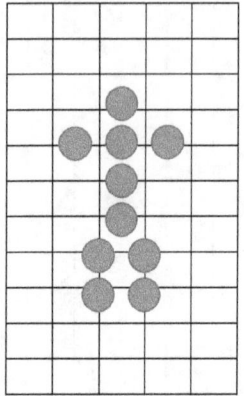

	One-Three-One-One-Two-Two	Two-Two-One-One-Three-One
Playing Orientation:	Neutral (5-5)	
No. of Strikers /Def players:	(1/2)	(2/1)
Shape:	Pentagon	
Shape spread:	(5X6)	
No. of half-side players (Neut):	7{(3(4)}	
No. of Outer players (Inner):	5 (5)	
No. of Mid-fielders (Neut):	7(0)	
No. of Att/Def Mid-fielders:	(4/3)	(3/4)

One-Three-One-One-Three-One

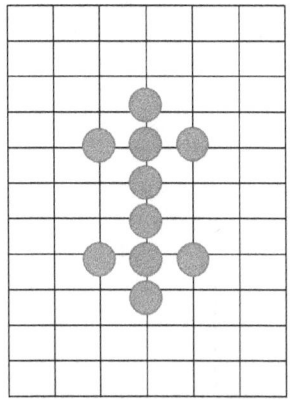

One-Three-One-One-Three-One

Playing Orientation:	Neutral (5-5)
No. of Strikers /Def players:	(1/1)
Shape:	Hexagon
Shape spread:	(3X6)
No. of half-side players (Neut):	8{(2(6)}
No. of Outer players (Inner):	6 (4)
No. of Mid-fielders (Neut):	8(0)
No. of Att/Def Mid-fielders:	(4/4)

One-Three-One-Two-One-Two and Two-One-Two-One-Three-One

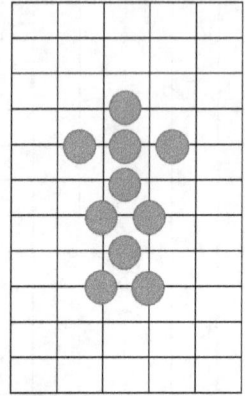

	One-Three-One-Two-One-Two	Two-One-Two-One-Three-One
Playing Orientation:	Neutral (5-5)	
No. of Strikers /Def players:	(1/2)	(2/1)
Shape:	Pentagon	
Shape spread:	(5X6)	
No. of half-side players (Neut):	7{(3(4)}	
No. of Outer players (Inner):	5 (5)	
No. of Mid-fielders (Neut):	7(0)	
No. of Att/Def Mid-fielders:	(4/3)	(3/4)

One-Three-Two-One-One-Two and Two-One-One-Two-Three-One

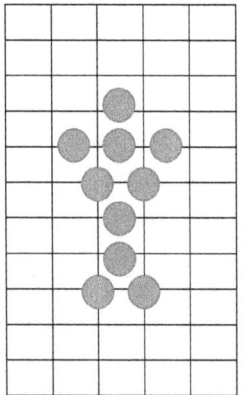

	One-Three-Two-One-One-Two	Two-One-One-Two-Three-One
Playing Orientation:	Attacking (4-6)	Defensive (6-4)
No. of Strikers /Def players:	(1/2)	(2/1)
Shape:	Pentagon	
Shape spread:	(5X6)	
No. of half-side players (Neut):	7{(3(4)}	
No. of Outer players (Inner):	5 (5)	
No. of Mid-fielders (Neut):	7(0)	
No. of Att/Def Mid-fielders:	(5/2)	(2/5)

One-Three-Two-Two-One-One and One-One-Two-Two-Three-One

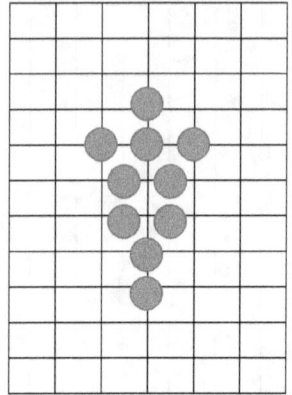

	One-Three-Two-Two-One-One	One-One-Two-Two-Three-One
Playing Orientation:	Attacking (4-6)	Defensive (6-4)
No. of Strikers /Def players:	(1/1)	(1/1)
Shape:	Quadrilateral	
Shape spread:	(5X6)	
No. of half-side players (Neut):	7{(3(4)}	
No. of Outer players (Inner):	6 (4)	
No. of Mid-fielders (Neut):	8(0)	
No. of Att/Def Mid-fielders:	(5/3)	(3/5)

One-Three-Three-One-One-One and One-One-One-Three-Three-One

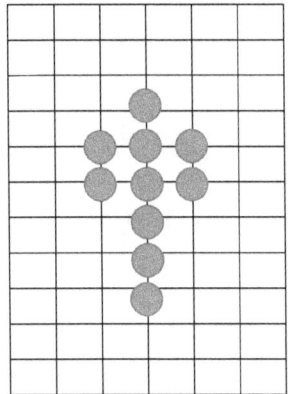

	One-Three-Three-One-One-One	One-One-One-Three-Three-One
Playing Orientation:	Attacking (3-7)	Defensive (7-3)
No. of Strikers /Def players:	(1/1)	(1/1)
Shape:	Hexagon	
Shape spread:	(3X6)	
No. of half-side players (Neut):	8{(2(6)}	
No. of Outer players (Inner):	6 (4)	
No. of Mid-fielders (Neut):	8(0)	
No. of Att/Def Mid-fielders:	(6/2)	(2/6)

One-Four-One-One-One-Two and Two-One-One-One-Four-One

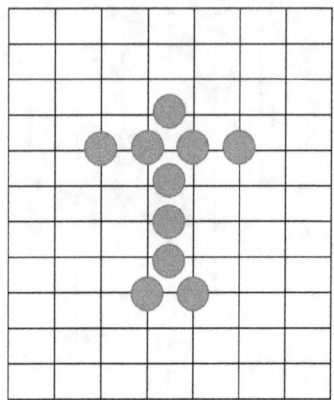

	One-Four-One-One-One-Two	Two-One-One-One-Four-One
Playing Orientation:	Attacking (4-6)	Defensive (6-4)
No. of Strikers /Def players:	(1/2)	(2/1)
Shape:	Pentagon	
Shape spread:	(5X6)	
No. of half-side players (Neut):	7{(3(4)}	
No. of Outer players (Inner):	5 (5)	
No. of Mid-fielders (Neut):	7(0)	
No. of Att/Def Mid-fielders:	(5/2)	(2/5)

One-Four-One-Two-One-One and One-One-Two-One-Four-One

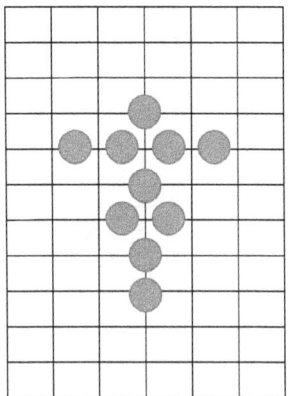

	One-Four-One-Two-One-One	One-One-Two-One-Four-One
Playing Orientation:	Attacking (4-6)	Defensive (6-4)
No. of Strikers /Def players:	(1/1)	(1/1)
Shape:	Quadrilateral	
Shape spread:	(5X6)	
No. of half-side players (Neut):	7{(3(4)}	
No. of Outer players (Inner):	4 (6)	
No. of Mid-fielders (Neut):	8(0)	
No. of Att/Def Mid-fielders:	(5/3)	(3/5)

One-Four-Two-One-One-One and One-One-One-Two-Four-One

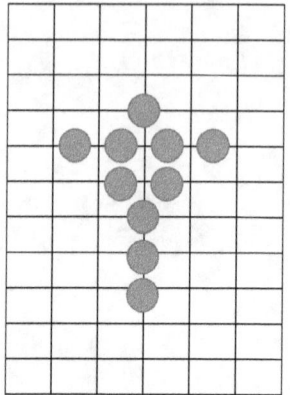

	One-Four-Two-One-One-One	One-One-One-Two-Four-One
Playing Orientation:	Attacking (3-7)	Defensive (7-3)
No. of Strikers /Def players:	(1/1)	(1/1)
Shape:	Quadrilateral	
Shape spread:	(5X6)	
No. of half-side players (Neut):	7{(3(4)}	
No. of Outer players (Inner):	4 (6)	
No. of Mid-fielders (Neut):	8(0)	
No. of Att/Def Mid-fielders:	(6/2)	(2/6)

Two-One-One-One-One-Four and Four-One-One-One-One-Two

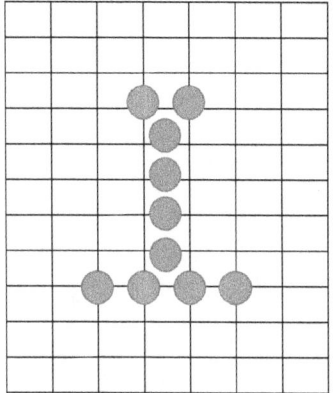

	Two-One-One-One-One-Four	Four-One-One-One-One-Two
Playing Orientation:	Defensive (6-4)	Attacking (4-6)
No. of Strikers /Def players:	(2/4)	(4/2)
Shape:	Trapezium	
Shape spread:	(5X6)	
No. of half-side players (Neut):	7{(3(4)}	
No. of Outer players (Inner):	6 (4)	
No. of Mid-fielders (Neut):	4(0)	
No. of Att/Def Mid-fielders:	(2/2)	(2/2)

Two-One-One-One-Two-Three and Three-Two-One-One-One-Two

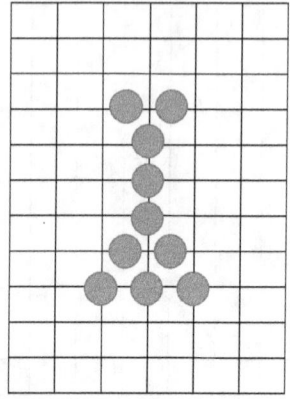

	Two-One-One-One-Two-Three	Three-Two-One-One-One-Two
Playing Orientation:	Defensive (6-4)	Attacking (4-6)
No. of Strikers /Def players:	(2/3)	(3/2)
Shape:	Trapezium	
Shape spread:	(5X6)	
No. of half-side players (Neut):	7{(3(4)}	
No. of Outer players (Inner):	5 (5)	
No. of Mid-fielders (Neut):	5(0)	
No. of Att/Def Mid-fielders:	(2/3)	(3/2)

Two-One-One-Two-One-Three and Three-One-Two-One-One-Two

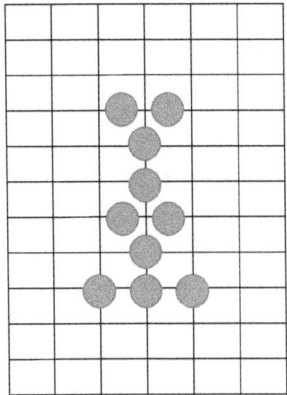

	Two-One-One-Two-One-Three	Three-One-Two-One-One-Two
Playing Orientation:	Defensive (6-4)	Attacking (4-6)
No. of Strikers /Def players:	(2/3)	(3/2)
Shape:	Trapezium	
Shape spread:	(5X6)	
No. of half-side players (Neut):	7{(3(4)}	
No. of Outer players (Inner):	5 (5)	
No. of Mid-fielders (Neut):	5(0)	
No. of Att/Def Mid-fielders:	(2/3)	(3/2)

Two-One-One-Two-Two-Two and Two-Two-Two-One-One-Two

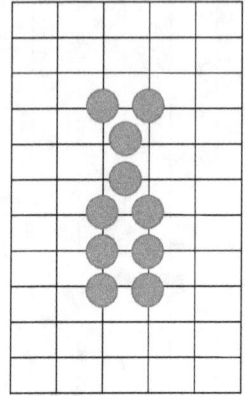

	Two-One-One-Two-Two-Two	Two-Two-Two-One-One-Two
Playing Orientation:	Defensive (6-4)	Attacking (4-6)
No. of Strikers /Def players:	(2/2)	(2/2)
Shape:	Rectangle	
Shape spread:	(3X6)	
No. of half-side players (Neut):	6{(4(2)}	
No. of Outer players (Inner):	8 (2)	
No. of Mid-fielders (Neut):	6(0)	
No. of Att/Def Mid-fielders:	(2/4)	(4/2)

Two-One-One-Three-One-Two and Two-One-Three-One-One-Two

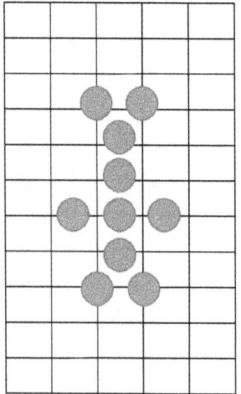

	Two-One-One-Three-One-Two	Two-One-Three-One-One-Two
Playing Orientation:	Defensive (6-4)	Attacking (4-6)
No. of Strikers /Def players:	(2/2)	(2/2)
Shape:	Hexagon	
Shape spread:	(5X6)	
No. of half-side players (Neut):	7{(3(4)}	
No. of Outer players (Inner):	6 (4)	
No. of Mid-fielders (Neut):	6(0)	
No. of Att/Def Mid-fielders:	(2/4)	(4/2)

Two-One-Two-One-One-Three and Three-One-One-Two-One-Two

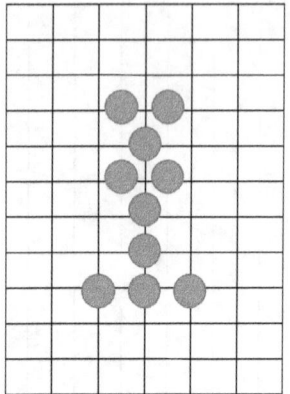

	Two-One-Two-One-One-Three	Three-One-One-Two-One-Two
Playing Orientation:	Neutral (5-5)	
No. of Strikers /Def players:	(2/3)	(3/2)
Shape:	Trapezium	
Shape spread:	(5X6)	
No. of half-side players (Neut):	7{(3(4)}	
No. of Outer players (Inner):	5 (5)	
No. of Mid-fielders (Neut):	5(0)	
No. of Att/Def Mid-fielders:	(3/2)	(2/3)

Two-One-Two-One-Two-Two and Two-Two-One-Two-One-Two

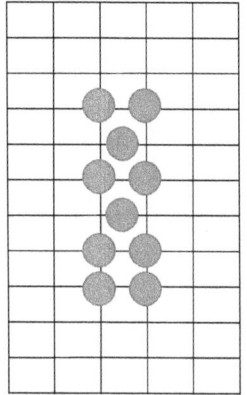

	Two-One-Two-One-Two-Two	Two-Two-One-Two-One-Two
Playing Orientation:	Neutral (5-5)	
No. of Strikers /Def players:	(2/2)	(2/2)
Shape:	Rectangle	
Shape spread:	(3X6)	
No. of half-side players (Neut):	6{(4(2)}	
No. of Outer players (Inner):	8 (2)	
No. of Mid-fielders (Neut):	6(0)	
No. of Att/Def Mid-fielders:	(3/3)	(3/3)

Two-One-Two-Two-One-Two

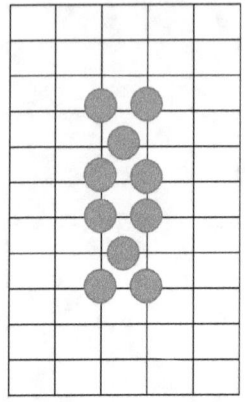

                                  Two-One-Two-Two-One-Two

Playing Orientation:	Neutral (5-5)
No. of Strikers /Def players:	(2/2)
Shape:	Rectangle
Shape spread:	(3X6)
No. of half-side players (Neut):	6{(4(2)}
No. of Outer players (Inner):	8 (2)
No. of Mid-fielders (Neut):	6(0)
No. of Att/Def Mid-fielders:	(3/3)

Two-Two-One-One-One-Three and Three-One-One-One-Two-Two

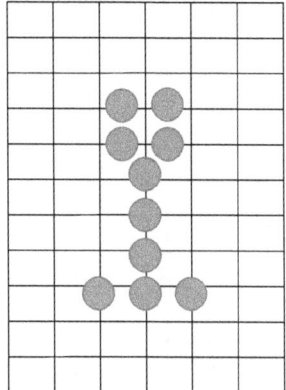

	Two-Two-One-One-One-Three	Three-One-One-One-Two-Two
Playing Orientation:	Neutral (5-5)	
No. of Strikers /Def players:	(2/3)	(3/2)
Shape:	Trapezium	
Shape spread:	(5X6)	
No. of half-side players (Neut):	7{(3(4)}	
No. of Outer players (Inner):	5 (5)	
No. of Mid-fielders (Neut):	5(0)	
No. of Att/Def Mid-fielders:	(3/2)	(2/3)

Two-Two-One-One-Two-Two

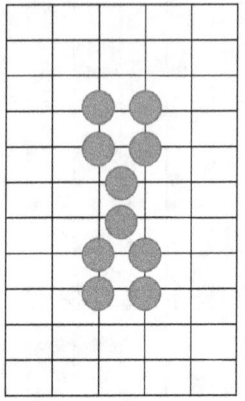

Two-Two-One-One-Two-Two

Playing Orientation:	Neutral (5-5)
No. of Strikers /Def players:	(2/2)
Shape:	Rectangle
Shape spread:	(3X6)
No. of half-side players (Neut):	6{(4(2)}
No. of Outer players (Inner):	8(2)
No. of Mid-fielders (Neut):	6(0)
No. of Att/Def Mid-fielders:	(3/3)

Two-Three-One-One-One-Two and Two-One-One-One-Three-Two

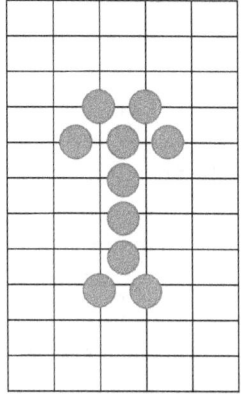

	Two-Three-One-One-One-Two	Two-One-One-One-Three-Two
Playing Orientation:	Attacking (4-6)	Defensive (6-4)
No. of Strikers /Def players:	(2/2)	(2/2)
Shape:	Hexagon	
Shape spread:	(5X6)	
No. of half-side players (Neut):	7{(3(4)}	
No. of Outer players (Inner):	6 (4)	
No. of Mid-fielders (Neut):	6(0)	
No. of Att/Def Mid-fielders:	(4/2)	(2/4)

Two-Three-One-Two-One-One and One-One-Two-One-Three-Two

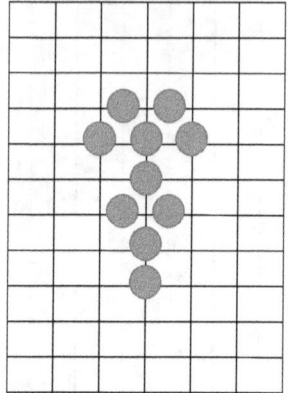

	Two-Three-One-Two-One-One	One-One-Two-One-Three-Two
Playing Orientation:	Attacking (4-6)	Defensive (6-4)
No. of Strikers /Def players:	(2/1)	(1/2)
Shape:	Pentagon	
Shape spread:	(5X6)	
No. of half-side players (Neut):	7{(3(4)}	
No. of Outer players (Inner):	5 (5)	
No. of Mid-fielders (Neut):	7(0)	
No. of Att/Def Mid-fielders:	(4/3)	(3/4)

Two-Three-Two-One-One-One and One-One-One-Two-Three-Two

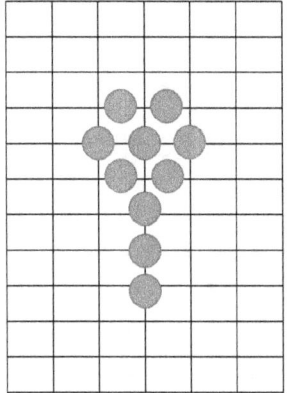

	Two-Three-Two-One-One-One	One-One-One-Two-Three-Two
Playing Orientation:	Attacking (3-7)	Defensive (7-3)
No. of Strikers /Def players:	(2/1)	(1/2)
Shape:	Pentagon	
Shape spread:	(5X6)	
No. of half-side players (Neut):	7{(3(4)}	
No. of Outer players (Inner):	5 (5)	
No. of Mid-fielders (Neut):	7(0)	
No. of Att/Def Mid-fielders:	(5/2)	(2/5)

Two-Four-One-One-One-One and One-One-One-One-Four-Two

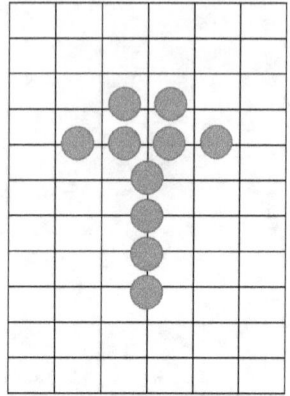

	Two-Four-One-One-One-One	One-One-One-One-Four-Two
Playing Orientation:	Attacking (3-7)	Defensive (7-3)
No. of Strikers /Def players:	(2/1)	(1/2)
Shape:	Pentagon	
Shape spread:	(5X6)	
No. of half-side players (Neut):	7{(3(4)}	
No. of Outer players (Inner):	5 (5)	
No. of Mid-fielders (Neut):	7(0)	
No. of Att/Def Mid-fielders:	(5/2)	(2/5)

Three-One-One-One-One-Three

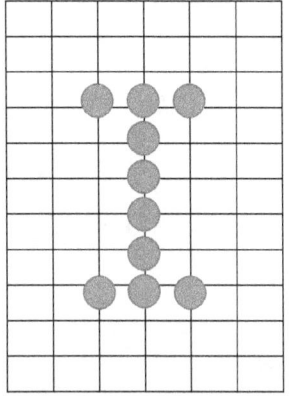

                                Three-One-One-One-One-Three

Playing Orientation:	Neutral (5-5)
No. of Strikers /Def players:	(3/3)
Shape:	Rectangle
Shape spread:	(3X6)
No. of half-side players (Neut):	8{(2(6)}
No. of Outer players (Inner):	6 (4)
No. of Mid-fielders (Neut):	4(0)
No. of Att/Def Mid-fielders:	(2/2)

LEVEL 7

Formations: 84

Symmetrically neutral: 4

One-One-One-One-One-One-Four and Four-One-One-One-One-One-One

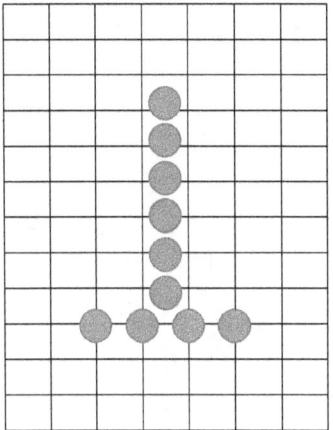

	One-One-One-One-One-One-Four	Four-One-One-One-One-One-One
Playing Orientation:	Defensive (7-4)	Attacking (4-7)
No. of Strikers /Def players:	(1/4)	(4/1)
Shape:	Triangle	
Shape spread:	(5X7)	
No. of half-side players (Neut):	8{(2(6)}	
No. of Outer players (Inner):	5 (5)	
No. of Mid-fielders (Neut):	5(1)	
No. of Att/Def Mid-fielders:	(2/2)	(2/2)

One-One-One-One-One-Two-Three and Three-Two-One-One-One-One-One

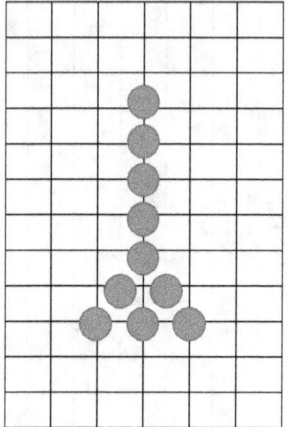

	One-One-One-One-One-Two-Three	Three-Two-One-One-One-One-One
Playing Orientation:	Defensive (7-4)	Attacking (4-7)
No. of Strikers /Def players:	(1/3)	(3/1)
Shape:	Triangle	
Shape spread:	(5X7)	
No. of half-side players (Neut):	8{(2(6)}	
No. of Outer players (Inner):	4 (6)	
No. of Mid-fielders (Neut):	6(1)	
No. of Att/Def Mid-fielders:	(2/3)	(3/2)

One-One-One-One-Two-One-Three and Three-One-Two-One-One-One-One

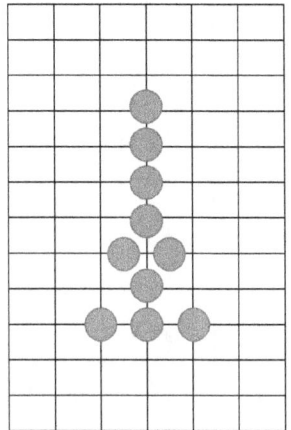

	One-One-One-One-Two-One-Three	Three-One-Two-One-One-One-One
Playing Orientation:	Defensive (7-4)	Attacking (4-7)
No. of Strikers /Def players:	(1/3)	(3/1)
Shape:	Triangle	
Shape spread:	(5X7)	
No. of half-side players (Neut):	8{(2(6)}	
No. of Outer players (Inner):	4 (6)	
No. of Mid-fielders (Neut):	6(1)	
No. of Att/Def Mid-fielders:	(2/3)	(3/2)

One-One-One-One-Two-Two-Two and Two-Two-Two-One-One-One-One

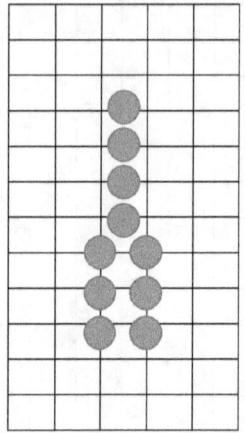

	One-One-One-One-Two-Two-Two	Two-Two-Two-One-One-One-One
Playing Orientation:	Defensive (7-4)	Attacking (4-7)
No. of Strikers /Def players:	(1/2)	(2/1)
Shape:	Pentagon	
Shape spread:	(3X7)	
No. of half-side players (Neut):	7{(3(4)}	
No. of Outer players (Inner):	7 (3)	
No. of Mid-fielders (Neut):	7(1)	
No. of Att/Def Mid-fielders:	(2/4)	(4/2)

One-One-One-One-Three-One-Two and Two-One-Three-One-One-One-One

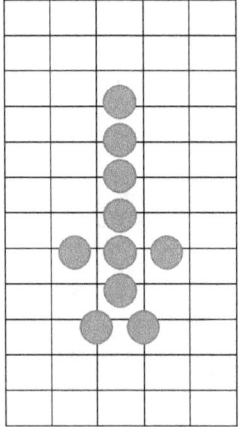

	One-One-One-One-Three-One-Two	Two-One-Three-One-One-One-One
Playing Orientation:	Defensive (7-4)	Attacking (4-7)
No. of Strikers /Def players:	(1/2)	(2/1)
Shape:	Pentagon	
Shape spread:	(5X7)	
No. of half-side players (Neut):	8{(2(6)}	
No. of Outer players (Inner):	5 (5)	
No. of Mid-fielders (Neut):	7(1)	
No. of Att/Def Mid-fielders:	(2/4)	(4/2)

One-One-One-Two-One-One-Three and Three-One-One-Two-One-One-One

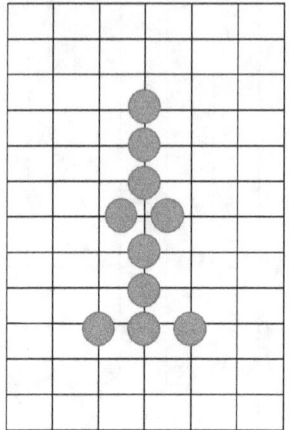

	One-One-One-Two-One-One-Three	Three-One-One-Two-One-One-One
Playing Orientation:	Defensive (7-5)	Attacking (5-7)
No. of Strikers /Def players:	(1/3)	(3/1)
Shape:	Triangle	
Shape spread:	(5X7)	
No. of half-side players (Neut):	8{(2(6)}	
No. of Outer players (Inner):	6 (4)	
No. of Mid-fielders (Neut):	6(2)	
No. of Att/Def Mid-fielders:	(2/2)	(2/2)

One-One-One-Two-One-Two-Two and Two-Two-One-Two-One-One-One

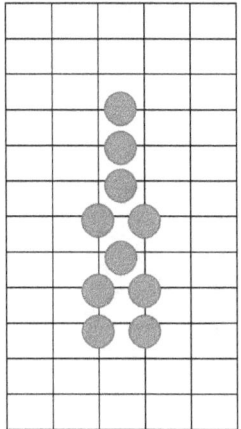

	One-One-One-Two-One-Two-Two	Two-Two-One-Two-One-One-One
Playing Orientation:	Defensive (7-5)	Attacking (5-7)
No. of Strikers /Def players:	(1/2)	(2/1)
Shape:	Pentagon	
Shape spread:	(3X7)	
No. of half-side players (Neut):	7{(3(4)}	
No. of Outer players (Inner):	7 (3)	
No. of Mid-fielders (Neut):	7(2)	
No. of Att/Def Mid-fielders:	(2/3)	(3/2)

One-One-One-Two-Two-One-Two and Two-One-Two-Two-One-One-One

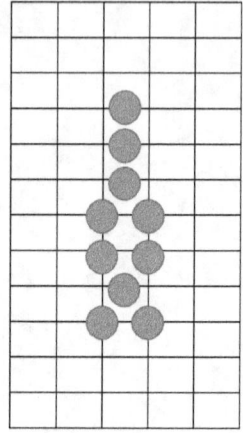

	One-One-One-Two-Two-One-Two	Two-One-Two-Two-One-One-One
Playing Orientation:	Defensive (7-5)	Attacking (5-7)
No. of Strikers /Def players:	(1/2)	(2/1)
Shape:	Pentagon	
Shape spread:	(3X7)	
No. of half-side players (Neut):	7{(3(4)}	
No. of Outer players (Inner):	7 (3)	
No. of Mid-fielders (Neut):	7(2)	
No. of Att/Def Mid-fielders:	(2/3)	(3/2)

One-One-One-Three-One-One-Two and Two-One-One-Three-One-One-One

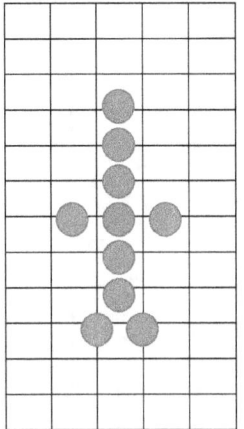

	One-One-One-Three-One-One-Two	Two-One-One-Three-One-One-One
Playing Orientation:	Defensive (7-6)	Attacking (6-7)
No. of Strikers /Def players:	(1/2)	(2/1)
Shape:	Pentagon	
Shape spread:	(5X7)	
No. of half-side players (Neut):	8{(2(6)}	
No. of Outer players (Inner):	5 (5)	
No. of Mid-fielders (Neut):	7(3)	
No. of Att/Def Mid-fielders:	(2/2)	(2/2)

One-One-One-Three-Two-One-One and One-One-Two-Three-One-One-One

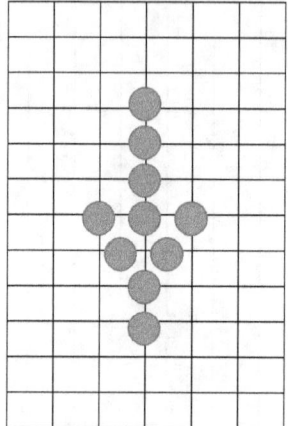

	One-One-One-Three-Two-One-One	One-One-Two-Three-One-One-One
Playing Orientation:	Defensive (7-6)	Attacking (6-7)
No. of Strikers /Def players:	(1/1)	(1/1)
Shape:	Quadrilateral	
Shape spread:	(5X7)	
No. of half-side players (Neut):	8{(2(6)}	
No. of Outer players (Inner):	4 (6)	
No. of Mid-fielders (Neut):	8(3)	
No. of Att/Def Mid-fielders:	(2/3)	(3/2)

One-One-One-Four-One-One-One

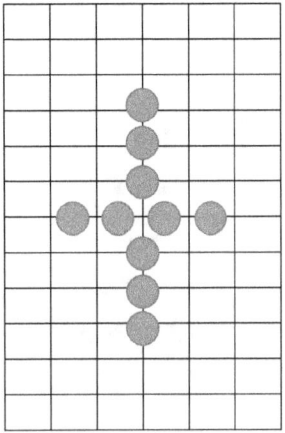

One-One-One-Four-One-One-One

Playing Orientation:	Neutral (7-7)
No. of Strikers /Def players:	(1/1)
Shape:	Quadrilateral
Shape spread:	(5X7)
No. of half-side players (Neut):	8{(2(6)}
No. of Outer players (Inner):	4 (6)
No. of Mid-fielders (Neut):	8(4)
No. of Att/Def Mid-fielders:	(2/2)

One-One-Two-One-One-One-Three and Three-One-One-One-Two-One-One

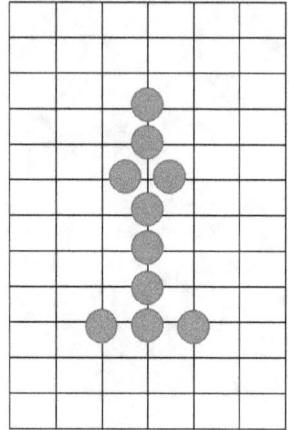

	One-One-Two-One-One-One-Three	Three-One-One-One-Two-One-One
Playing Orientation:	Defensive (6-5)	Attacking (5-6)
No. of Strikers /Def players:	(1/3)	(3/1)
Shape:	Pentagon	
Shape spread:	(5X7)	
No. of half-side players (Neut):	8{(2(6)}	
No. of Outer players (Inner):	6 (4)	
No. of Mid-fielders (Neut):	6(1)	
No. of Att/Def Mid-fielders:	(3/2)	(2/3)

One-One-Two-One-One-Two-Two and Two-Two-One-One-Two-One-One

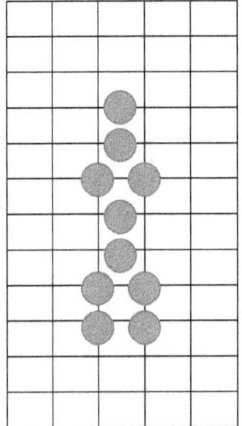

	One-One-Two-One-One-Two-Two	Two-Two-One-One-Two-One-One
Playing Orientation:	Defensive (6-5)	Attacking (5-6)
No. of Strikers /Def players:	(1/2)	(2/1)
Shape:	Pentagon	
Shape spread:	(3X7)	
No. of half-side players (Neut):	7{(3(4)}	
No. of Outer players (Inner):	7 (3)	
No. of Mid-fielders (Neut):	7(1)	
No. of Att/Def Mid-fielders:	(3/3)	(3/3)

One-One-Two-One-Two-One-Two and Two-One-Two-One-Two-One-One

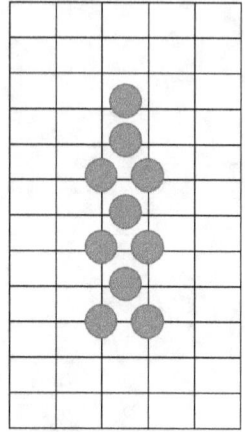

	One-One-Two-One-Two-One-Two	Two-One-Two-One-Two-One-One
Playing Orientation:	Defensive (6-5)	Attacking (5-6)
No. of Strikers /Def players:	(1/2)	(2/1)
Shape:	Pentagon	
Shape spread:	(3X7)	
No. of half-side players (Neut):	7{(3(4)}	
No. of Outer players (Inner):	7 (3)	
No. of Mid-fielders (Neut):	7(1)	
No. of Att/Def Mid-fielders:	(3/3)	(3/3)

One-One-Two-Two-One-One-Two and Two-One-One-Two-Two-One-One

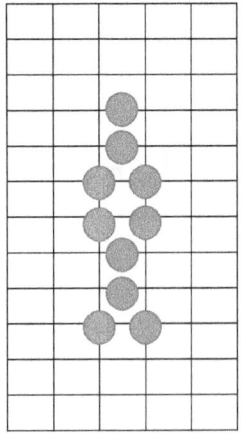

	One-One-Two-Two-One-One-Two	Two-One-One-Two-Two-One-One
Playing Orientation:	Neutral (6-6)	
No. of Strikers /Def players:	(1/2)	(2/1)
Shape:	Pentagon	
Shape spread:	(3X7)	
No. of half-side players (Neut):	7{(3(4)}	
No. of Outer players (Inner):	7 (3)	
No. of Mid-fielders (Neut):	7(2)	
No. of Att/Def Mid-fielders:	(3/2)	(2/3)

One-One-Two-Two-Two-One-One

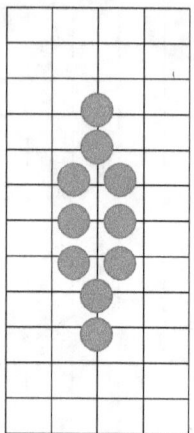

One-One-Two-Two-Two-One-One

Playing Orientation:	Neutral (6-6)
No. of Strikers /Def players:	(1/1)
Shape:	Hexagon
Shape spread:	(3X7)
No. of half-side players (Neut):	7{(3(4)}
No. of Outer players (Inner):	8 (2)
No. of Mid-fielders (Neut):	8(2)
No. of Att/Def Mid-fielders:	(3/3)

One-One-Three-One-One-One-Two and Two-One-One-One-Three-One-One

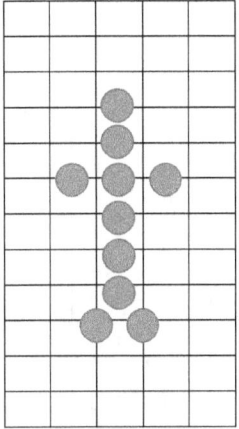

	One-One-Three-One-One-One-Two	Two-One-One-One-Three-One-One
Playing Orientation:	Attacking (5-6)	Defensive (6-5)
No. of Strikers /Def players:	(1/2)	(2/1)
Shape:	Pentagon	
Shape spread:	(5X7)	
No. of half-side players (Neut):	8{(2(6)}	
No. of Outer players (Inner):	5 (5)	
No. of Mid-fielders (Neut):	7(1)	
No. of Att/Def Mid-fielders:	(4/2)	(2/4)

One-One-Three-One-One-Two-One and One-Two-One-One-Three-One-One

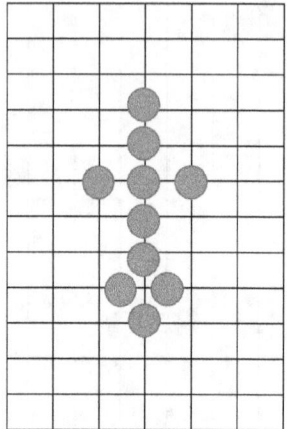

	One-One-Three-One-One-Two-One	One-Two-One-One-Three-One-One
Playing Orientation:	Attacking (5-6)	Defensive (6-5)
No. of Strikers /Def players:	(1/1)	(1/1)
Shape:	Hexagon	
Shape spread:	(5X7)	
No. of half-side players (Neut):	8{(2(6)}	
No. of Outer players (Inner):	6 (4)	
No. of Mid-fielders (Neut):	8(1)	
No. of Att/Def Mid-fielders:	(4/3)	(3/4)

One-One-Three-One-Two-One-One and One-One-Two-One-Three-One-One

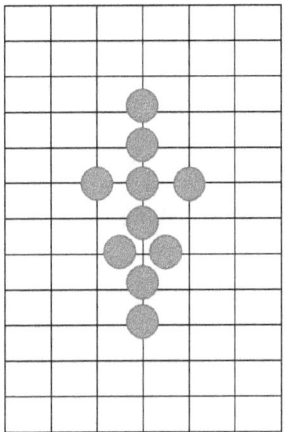

	One-One-Three-One-Two-One-One	One-One-Two-One-Three-One-One
Playing Orientation:	Attacking (5-6)	Defensive (6-5)
No. of Strikers /Def players:	(1/1)	(1/1)
Shape:	Quadrilateral	
Shape spread:	(5X7)	
No. of half-side players (Neut):	8{(2(6)}	
No. of Outer players (Inner):	6 (4)	
No. of Mid-fielders (Neut):	8(1)	
No. of Att/Def Mid-fielders:	(4/3)	(3/4)

One-One-Three-Two-One-One-One and One-One-One-Two-Three-One-One

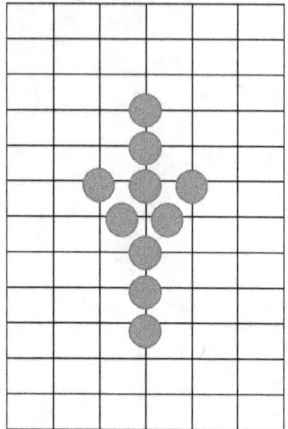

	One-One-Three-Two-One-One-One	One-One-One-Two-Three-One-One
Playing Orientation:	Attacking (5-7)	Defensive (7-5)
No. of Strikers /Def players:	(1/1)	(1/1)
Shape:	Quadrilateral	
Shape spread:	(5X7)	
No. of half-side players (Neut):	8{(2(6)}	
No. of Outer players (Inner):	4 (6)	
No. of Mid-fielders (Neut):	8(2)	
No. of Att/Def Mid-fielders:	(4/2)	(2/4)

One-One-Four-One-One-One-One and One-One-One-One-Four-One-One

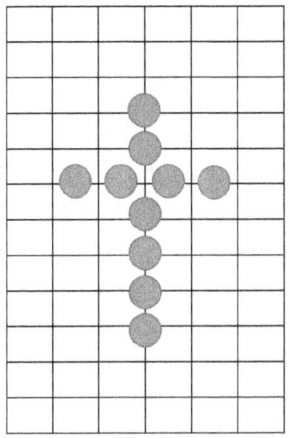

	One-One-Four-One-One-One-One	One-One-One-One-Four-One-One
Playing Orientation:	Attacking (4-7)	Defensive (7-4)
No. of Strikers /Def players:	(1/1)	(1/1)
Shape:	Quadrilateral	
Shape spread:	(5X7)	
No. of half-side players (Neut):	8{(2(6)}	
No. of Outer players (Inner):	4 (6)	
No. of Mid-fielders (Neut):	8(1)	
No. of Att/Def Mid-fielders:	(5/2)	(2/5)

One-Two-One-One-One-One-Three and Three-One-One-One-One-Two-One

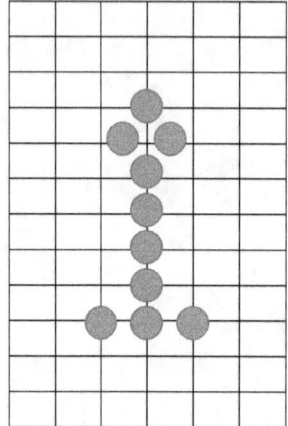

	One-Two-One-One-One-One-Three	Three-One-One-One-One-Two-One
Playing Orientation:	Defensive (6-5)	Attacking (5-6)
No. of Strikers /Def players:	(1/3)	(3/1)
Shape:	Pentagon	
Shape spread:	(5X7)	
No. of half-side players (Neut):	8{(2(6)}	
No. of Outer players (Inner):	6 (4)	
No. of Mid-fielders (Neut):	6(1)	
No. of Att/Def Mid-fielders:	(3/2)	(2/3)

One-Two-One-One-One-Two-Two and Two-Two-One-One-One-Two-One

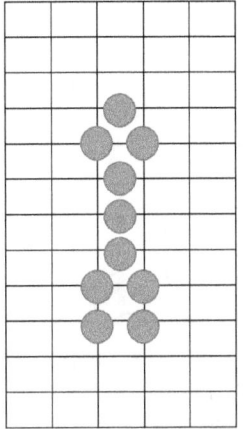

	One-Two-One-One-One-Two-Two	Two-Two-One-One-One-Two-One
Playing Orientation:	Defensive (6-5)	Attacking (5-6)
No. of Strikers /Def players:	(1/2)	(2/1)
Shape:	Pentagon	
Shape spread:	(3X7)	
No. of half-side players (Neut):	7{(3(4)}	
No. of Outer players (Inner):	7 (3)	
No. of Mid-fielders (Neut):	7(1)	
No. of Att/Def Mid-fielders:	(3/3)	(3/3)

One-Two-One-One-One-Three-One and One-Three-One-One-One-Two-One

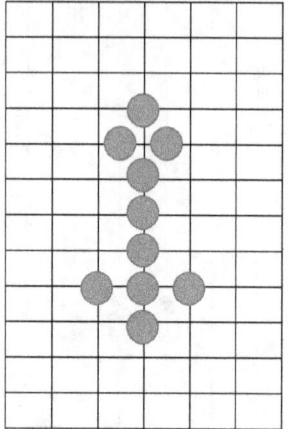

	One-Two-One-One-One-Three-One	One-Three-One-One-One-Two-One
Playing Orientation:	Defensive (6-5)	Attacking (5-6)
No. of Strikers /Def players:	(1/1)	(1/1)
Shape:	Hexagon	
Shape spread:	(5X7)	
No. of half-side players (Neut):	8{(2(6)}	
No. of Outer players (Inner):	6 (4)	
No. of Mid-fielders (Neut):	8(1)	
No. of Att/Def Mid-fielders:	(3/4)	(4/3)

One-Two-One-One-Two-One-Two and Two-One-Two-One-One-Two-One

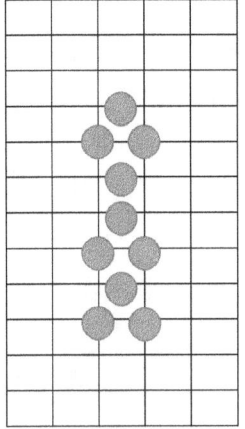

	One-Two-One-One-Two-One-Two	Two-One-Two-One-One-Two-One
Playing Orientation:	Defensive (6-5)	Attacking (5-6)
No. of Strikers /Def players:	(1/2)	(2/1)
Shape:	Pentagon	
Shape spread:	(3X7)	
No. of half-side players (Neut):	7{(3(4)}	
No. of Outer players (Inner):	7 (3)	
No. of Mid-fielders (Neut):	7(1)	
No. of Att/Def Mid-fielders:	(3/3)	(3/3)

One-Two-One-One-Two-Two-One and One-Two-Two-One-One-Two-One

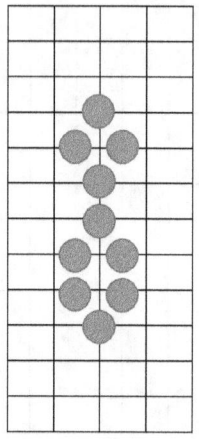

	One-Two-One-One-Two-Two-One	One-Two-Two-One-One-Two-One
Playing Orientation:	Defensive (6-5)	Attacking (5-6)
No. of Strikers /Def players:	(1/1)	(1/1)
Shape:	Hexagon	
Shape spread:	(3X7)	
No. of half-side players (Neut):	7{(3(4)}	
No. of Outer players (Inner):	8 (2)	
No. of Mid-fielders (Neut):	8(1)	
No. of Att/Def Mid-fielders:	(3/4)	(4/3)

One-Two-One-Two-One-One-Two and Two-One-One-Two-One-Two-One

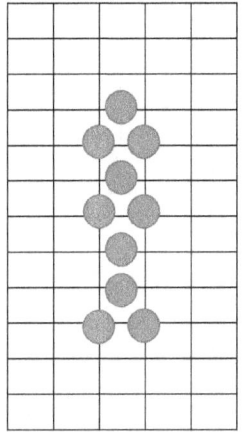

	One-Two-One-Two-One-One-Two	Two-One-One-Two-One-Two-One
Playing Orientation:	Neutral (6-6)	
No. of Strikers /Def players:	(1/2)	(2/1)
Shape:	Pentagon	
Shape spread:	(3X7)	
No. of half-side players (Neut):	7{(3(4)}	
No. of Outer players (Inner):	7 (3)	
No. of Mid-fielders (Neut):	7(2)	
No. of Att/Def Mid-fielders:	(3/2)	(2/3)

One-Two-One-Two-One-Two-One

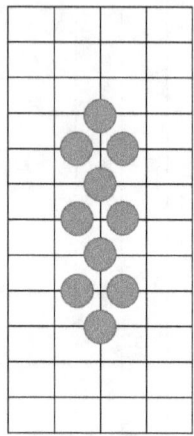

                        One-Two-One-Two-One-Two-One

Playing Orientation:	Neutral (6-6)
No. of Strikers /Def players:	(1/1)
Shape:	Hexagon
Shape spread:	(3X7)
No. of half-side players (Neut):	7{(3(4)}
No. of Outer players (Inner):	8 (2)
No. of Mid-fielders (Neut):	8(2)
No. of Att/Def Mid-fielders:	(3/3)

One-Two-One-Two-Two-One-One and One-One-Two-Two-One-Two-One

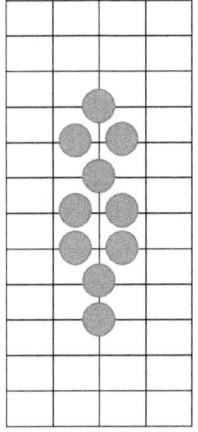

	One-Two-One-Two-Two-One-One	One-One-Two-Two-One-Two-One
Playing Orientation:	Neutral (6-6)	
No. of Strikers /Def players:	(1/1)	(1/1)
Shape:	Hexagon	
Shape spread:	(3X7)	
No. of half-side players (Neut):	7{(3(4)}	
No. of Outer players (Inner):	8 (2)	
No. of Mid-fielders (Neut):	8(2)	
No. of Att/Def Mid-fielders:	(3/3)	(3/3)

One-Two-One-Three-One-One-One and One-One-One-Three-One-Two-One

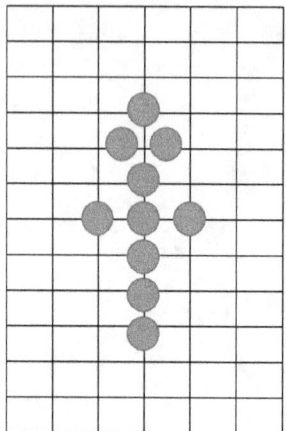

	One-Two-One-Three-One-One-One	One-One-One-Three-One-Two-One
Playing Orientation:	Attacking (6-7)	Defensive (7-6)
No. of Strikers /Def players:	(1/1)	(1/1)
Shape:	Hexagon	
Shape spread:	(5X7)	
No. of half-side players (Neut):	8{(2(6)}	
No. of Outer players (Inner):	6 (4)	
No. of Mid-fielders (Neut):	8(3)	
No. of Att/Def Mid-fielders:	(3/2)	(2/3)

One-Two-Two-One-One-One-Two and Two-One-One-One-Two-Two-One

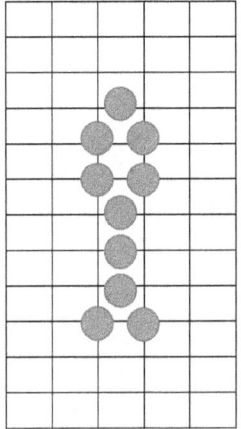

	One-Two-Two-One-One-One-Two	Two-One-One-One-Two-Two-One
Playing Orientation:	Attacking (5-6)	Defensive (6-5)
No. of Strikers /Def players:	(1/2)	(2/1)
Shape:	Pentagon	
Shape spread:	(3X7)	
No. of half-side players (Neut):	7{(3(4)}	
No. of Outer players (Inner):	7 (3)	
No. of Mid-fielders (Neut):	7(1)	
No. of Att/Def Mid-fielders:	(4/2)	(2/4)

One-Two-Two-One-Two-One-One and One-One-Two-One-Two-Two-One

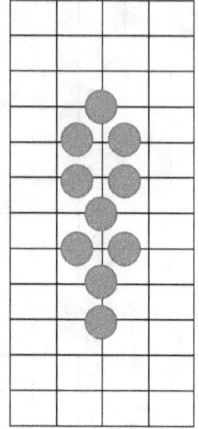

	One-Two-Two-One-Two-One-One	One-One-Two-One-Two-Two-One
Playing Orientation:	Attacking (5-6)	Defensive (6-5)
No. of Strikers /Def players:	(1/1)	(1/1)
Shape:	Hexagon	
Shape spread:	(3X7)	
No. of half-side players (Neut):	7{(3(4)}	
No. of Outer players (Inner):	8 (2)	
No. of Mid-fielders (Neut):	8(1)	
No. of Att/Def Mid-fielders:	(4/3)	(3/4)

One-Two-Two-Two-One-One-One and One-One-One-Two-Two-Two-One

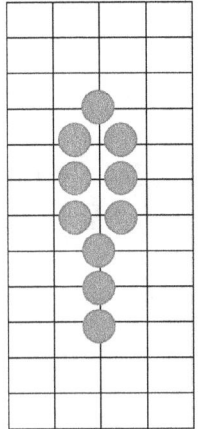

	One-Two-Two-Two-One-One-One	One-One-One-Two-Two-Two-One
Playing Orientation:	Attacking (5-7)	Defensive (7-5)
No. of Strikers /Def players:	(1/1)	(1/1)
Shape:	Hexagon	
Shape spread:	(3X7)	
No. of half-side players (Neut):	7{(3(4)}	
No. of Outer players (Inner):	8 (2)	
No. of Mid-fielders (Neut):	8(2)	
No. of Att/Def Mid-fielders:	(4/2)	(2/4)

One-Two-Three-One-One-One-One and One-One-One-One-Three-Two-One

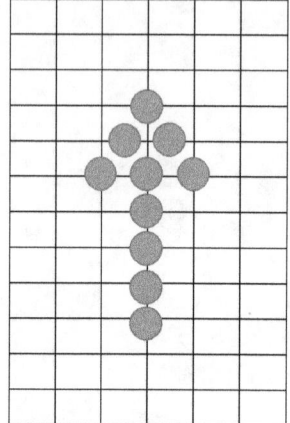

	One-Two-Three-One-One-One-One	One-One-One-One-Three-Two-One
Playing Orientation:	Attacking (4-7)	Defensive (7-4)
No. of Strikers /Def players:	(1/1)	(1/1)
Shape:	Quadrilateral	
Shape spread:	(5X7)	
No. of half-side players (Neut):	8{(2(6)}	
No. of Outer players (Inner):	6 (4)	
No. of Mid-fielders (Neut):	8(1)	
No. of Att/Def Mid-fielders:	(5/2)	(2/5)

One-Three-One-One-One-One-Two and Two-One-One-One-One-Three-One

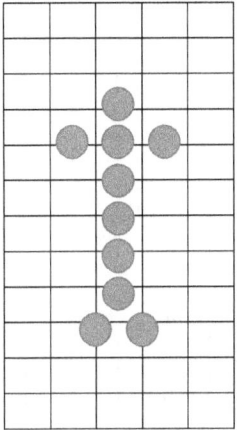

	One-Three-One-One-One-One-Two	Two-One-One-One-One-Three-One
Playing Orientation:	Attacking (5-6)	Defensive (6-5)
No. of Strikers /Def players:	(1/2)	(2/1)
Shape:	Pentagon	
Shape spread:	(5X7)	
No. of half-side players (Neut):	8{(2(6)}	
No. of Outer players (Inner):	5 (5)	
No. of Mid-fielders (Neut):	7(1)	
No. of Att/Def Mid-fielders:	(4/2)	(2/4)

One-Three-One-One-Two-One-One and One-One-Two-One-One-Three-One

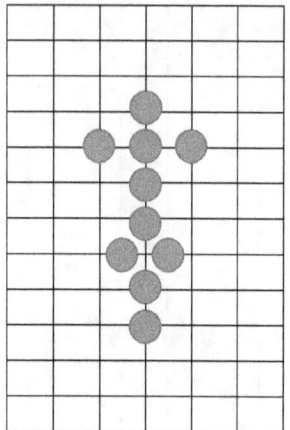

	One-Three-One-One-Two-One-One	One-One-Two-One-One-Three-One
Playing Orientation:	Attacking (5-6)	Defensive (6-5)
No. of Strikers /Def players:	(1/1)	(1/1)
Shape:	Hexagon	
Shape spread:	(5X7)	
No. of half-side players (Neut):	8{(2(6)}	
No. of Outer players (Inner):	6 (4)	
No. of Mid-fielders (Neut):	8(1)	
No. of Att/Def Mid-fielders:	(4/3)	(3/4)

One-Three-One-Two-One-One-One and One-One-One-Two-One-Three-One

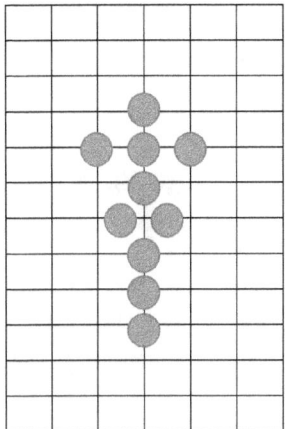

	One-Three-One-Two-One-One-One	One-One-One-Two-One-Three-One
Playing Orientation:	Attacking (5-7)	Defensive (7-5)
No. of Strikers /Def players:	(1/1)	(1/1)
Shape:	Quadrilateral	
Shape spread:	(5X7)	
No. of half-side players (Neut):	8{(2(6)}	
No. of Outer players (Inner):	4 (6)	
No. of Mid-fielders (Neut):	8(2)	
No. of Att/Def Mid-fielders:	(4/2)	(2/4)

One-Three-Two-One-One-One-One and One-One-One-One-Two-Three-One

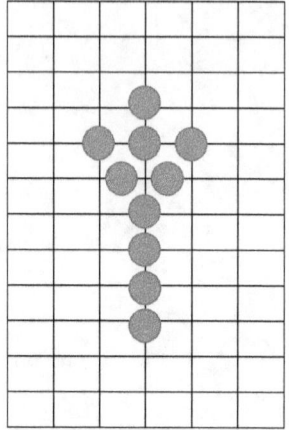

	One-Three-Two-One-One-One-One	One-One-One-One-Two-Three-One
Playing Orientation:	Attacking (4-7)	Defensive (7-4)
No. of Strikers /Def players:	(1/1)	(1/1)
Shape:	Quadrilateral	
Shape spread:	(5X7)	
No. of half-side players (Neut):	8{(2(6)}	
No. of Outer players (Inner):	4 (6)	
No. of Mid-fielders (Neut):	8(1)	
No. of Att/Def Mid-fielders:	(5/2)	(2/5)

One-Four-One-One-One-One-One and One-One-One-One-One-Four-One

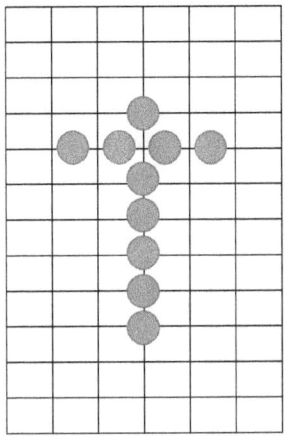

	One-Four-One-One-One-One-One	One-One-One-One-One-Four-One
Playing Orientation:	Attacking (4-7)	Defensive (7-4)
No. of Strikers /Def players:	(1/1)	(1/1)
Shape:	Quadrilateral	
Shape spread:	(5X7)	
No. of half-side players (Neut):	8{(2(6)}	
No. of Outer players (Inner):	4 (6)	
No. of Mid-fielders (Neut):	8(1)	
No. of Att/Def Mid-fielders:	(5/2)	(2/5)

Two-One-One-One-One-One-Three and Three-One-One-One-One-One-Two

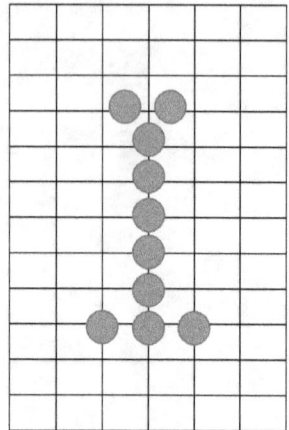

	Two-One-One-One-One-One-Three	Three-One-One-One-One-One-Two
Playing Orientation:	Defensive (6-5)	Attacking (5-6)
No. of Strikers /Def players:	(2/3)	(3/2)
Shape:	Trapezium	
Shape spread:	(5X7)	
No. of half-side players (Neut):	8{(2(6)}	
No. of Outer players (Inner):	5 (5)	
No. of Mid-fielders (Neut):	5(1)	
No. of Att/Def Mid-fielders:	(2/2)	(2/2)

Two-One-One-One-One-Two-Two and Two-Two-One-One-One-One-Two

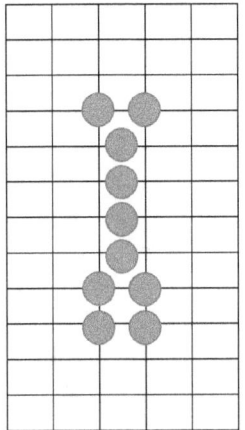

	Two-One-One-One-One-Two-Two	Two-Two-One-One-One-One-Two
Playing Orientation:	Defensive (6-5)	Attacking (5-6)
No. of Strikers /Def players:	(2/2)	(2/2)
Shape:	Rectangle	
Shape spread:	(3X7)	
No. of half-side players (Neut):	7{(3(4)}	
No. of Outer players (Inner):	6 (4)	
No. of Mid-fielders (Neut):	6(1)	
No. of Att/Def Mid-fielders:	(2/3)	(3/2)

Two-One-One-One-Two-One-Two and Two-One-Two-One-One-One-Two

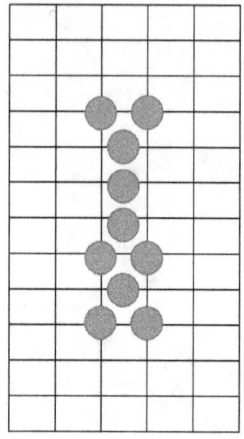

	Two-One-One-One-Two-One-Two	Two-One-Two-One-One-One-Two
Playing Orientation:	Defensive (6-5)	Attacking (5-6)
No. of Strikers /Def players:	(2/2)	(2/2)
Shape:	Rectangle	
Shape spread:	(3X7)	
No. of half-side players (Neut):	7{(3(4)}	
No. of Outer players (Inner):	6 (4)	
No. of Mid-fielders (Neut):	6(1)	
No. of Att/Def Mid-fielders:	(2/3)	(3/2)

Two-One-One-Two-One-One-Two

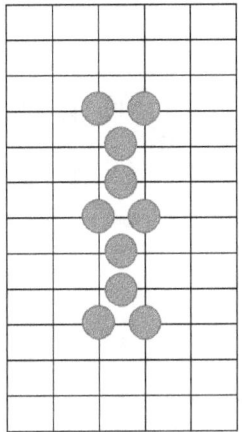

Two-One-One-Two-One-One-Two

Playing Orientation:	Neutral (6-6)
No. of Strikers /Def players:	(2/2)
Shape:	Rectangle
Shape spread:	(3X7)
No. of half-side players (Neut):	7{(3(4)}
No. of Outer players (Inner):	6 (4)
No. of Mid-fielders (Neut):	6(2)
No. of Att/Def Mid-fielders:	(2/2)

Two-Three-One-One-One-One-One and One-One-One-One-One-Three-Two

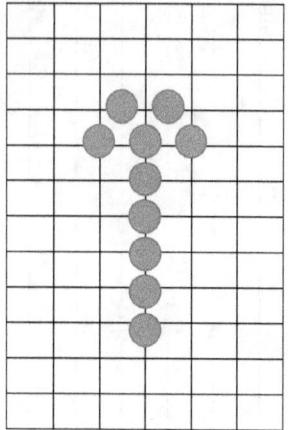

	Two-Three-One-One-One-One-One	One-One-One-One-One-Three-Two
Playing Orientation:	Attacking (4-7)	Defensive (7-4)
No. of Strikers /Def players:	(2/1)	(1/2)
Shape:	Pentagon	
Shape spread:	(5X7)	
No. of half-side players (Neut):	8{(2(6)}	
No. of Outer players (Inner):	5 (5)	
No. of Mid-fielders (Neut):	7(1)	
No. of Att/Def Mid-fielders:	(4/2)	(2/4)

LEVEL 8

Formations: 36

Symmetrically neutral: 4

One-One-One-One-One-One-One-Three and Three-One-One-One-One-One-One-One

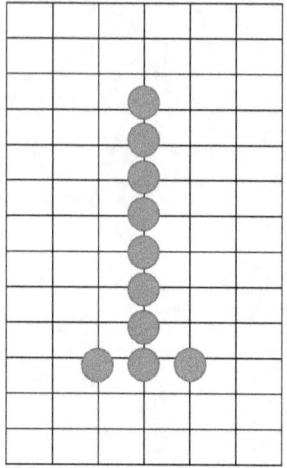

	One-One-One-One-One-One-One-Three	Three-One-One-One-One-One-One-One
Playing Orientation:	Defensive (6-4)	Attacking (4-6)
No. of Strikers /Def players:	(1/3)	(3/1)
Shape:	Triangle	
Shape spread:	(3X8)	
No. of half-side players (Neut):	9{(1(8)}	
No. of Outer players (Inner):	4 (6)	
No. of Mid-fielders (Neut):	6(0)	
No. of Att/Def Mid-fielders:	(3/3)	(3/3)

One-One-One-One-One-One-Two-Two and Two-Two-One-One-One-One-One-One

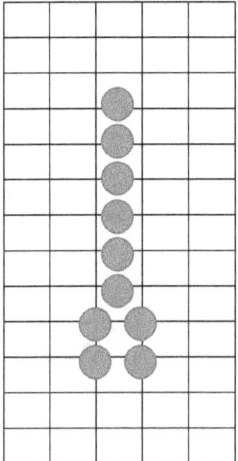

	One-One-One-One-One-One-Two-Two	Two-Two-One-One-One-One-One-One
Playing Orientation:	Defensive (6-4)	Attacking (4-6)
No. of Strikers /Def players:	(1/2)	(2/1)
Shape:	Pentagon	
Shape spread:	(3X8)	
No. of half-side players (Neut):	8{(2(6)}	
No. of Outer players (Inner):	5 (5)	
No. of Mid-fielders (Neut):	7(0)	
No. of Att/Def Mid-fielders:	(3/4)	(4/3)

One-One-One-One-One-Two-One-Two and Two-One-Two-One-One-One-One-One

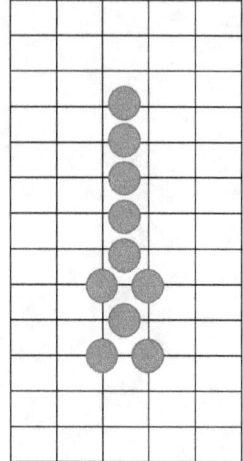

	One-One-One-One-One-Two-One-Two	Two-One-Two-One-One-One-One-One
Playing Orientation:	Defensive (6-4)	Attacking (4-6)
No. of Strikers /Def players:	(1/2)	(2/1)
Shape:	Pentagon	
Shape spread:	(3X8)	
No. of half-side players (Neut):	8{(2(6)}	
No. of Outer players (Inner):	5 (5)	
No. of Mid-fielders (Neut):	7(0)	
No. of Att/Def Mid-fielders:	(3/4)	(4/3)

One-One-One-One-Two-One-One-Two and Two-One-One-Two-One-One-One-One

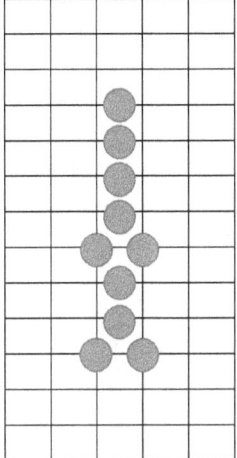

	One-One-One-One-Two-One-One-Two	Two-One-One-Two-One-One-One-One
Playing Orientation:	Defensive (6-4)	Attacking (4-6)
No. of Strikers /Def players:	(1/2)	(2/1)
Shape:	Pentagon	
Shape spread:	(3X8)	
No. of half-side players (Neut):	8{(2(6)}	
No. of Outer players (Inner):	5 (5)	
No. of Mid-fielders (Neut):	7(0)	
No. of Att/Def Mid-fielders:	(3/4)	(4/3)

One-One-One-One-Two-Two-One-One and One-One-Two-Two-One-One-One-One

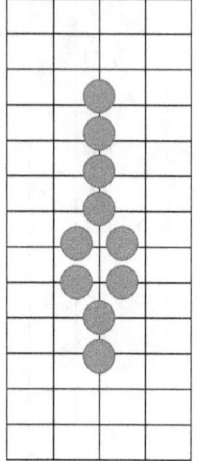

	One-One-One-One-Two-Two-One-One	One-One-Two-Two-One-One-One-One
Playing Orientation:	Defensive (6-4)	Attacking (4-6)
No. of Strikers /Def players:	(1/1)	(1/1)
Shape:	Hexagon	
Shape spread:	(3X8)	
No. of half-side players (Neut):	8{(2(6)}	
No. of Outer players (Inner):	6 (4)	
No. of Mid-fielders (Neut):	8(0)	
No. of Att/Def Mid-fielders:	(3/5)	(5/3)

One-One-One-One-Three-One-One-One and One-One-One-Three-One-One-One-One

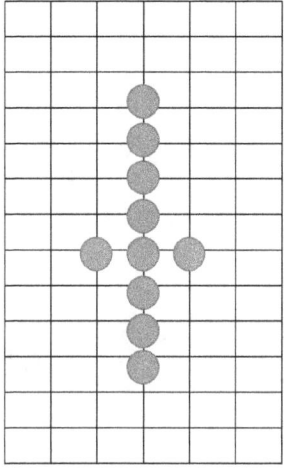

	One-One-One-One-Three-One-One-One	One-One-One-Three-One-One-One-One
Playing Orientation:	Defensive (6-4)	Attacking (4-6)
No. of Strikers /Def players:	(1/1)	(1/1)
Shape:	Quadrilateral	
Shape spread:	(3X8)	
No. of half-side players (Neut):	9{(1(8)}	
No. of Outer players (Inner):	4 (6)	
No. of Mid-fielders (Neut):	8(0)	
No. of Att/Def Mid-fielders:	(3/5)	(5/3)

One-One-One-Two-One-One-One-Two and Two-One-One-One-Two-One-One-One

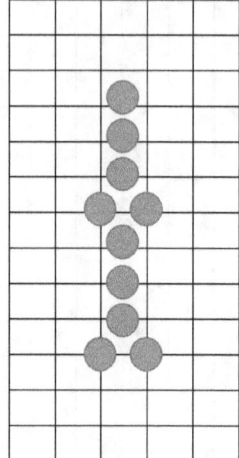

	One-One-One-Two-One-One-One-Two	Two-One-One-One-Two-One-One-One
Playing Orientation:	Neutral (5-5)	
No. of Strikers /Def players:	(1/2)	(2/1)
Shape:	Pentagon	
Shape spread:	(3X8)	
No. of half-side players (Neut):	8{(2(6)}	
No. of Outer players (Inner):	5 (5)	
No. of Mid-fielders (Neut):	7(0)	
No. of Att/Def Mid-fielders:	(4/3)	(3/4)

One-One-One-Two-One-Two-One-One and One-One-Two-One-Two-One-One-One

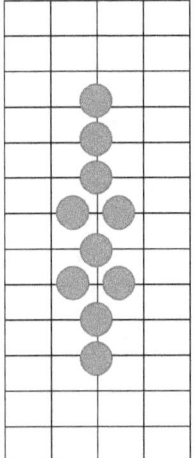

	One-One-One-Two-One-Two-One-One	One-One-Two-One-Two-One-One-One
Playing Orientation:	Neutral (5-5)	
No. of Strikers /Def players:	(1/1)	(1/1)
Shape:	Hexagon	
Shape spread:	(3X8)	
No. of half-side players (Neut):	8{(2(6)}	
No. of Outer players (Inner):	6 (4)	
No. of Mid-fielders (Neut):	8(0)	
No. of Att/Def Mid-fielders:	(4/4)	(4/4)

One-One-One-Two-Two-One-One-One

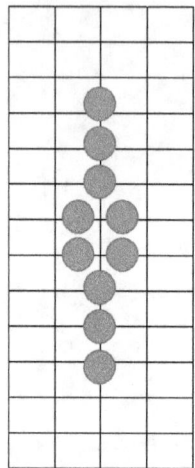

	One-One-One-Two-Two-One-One-One
Playing Orientation:	Neutral (5-5)
No. of Strikers /Def players:	(1/1)
Shape:	Hexagon
Shape spread:	(3X8)
No. of half-side players (Neut):	8{(2(6)}
No. of Outer players (Inner):	6 (4)
No. of Mid-fielders (Neut):	8(0)
No. of Att/Def Mid-fielders:	(4/4)

One-One-Two-One-One-One-One-Two and Two-One-One-One-One-Two-One-One

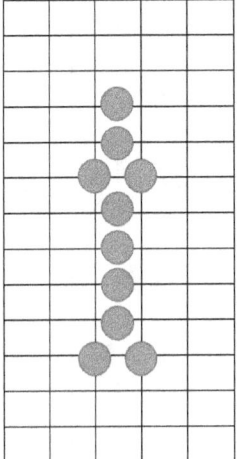

	One-One-Two-One-One-One-One-Two	Two-One-One-One-One-Two-One-One
Playing Orientation:	Neutral (5-5)	
No. of Strikers /Def players:	(1/2)	(2/1)
Shape:	Pentagon	
Shape spread:	(3X8)	
No. of half-side players (Neut):	8{(2(6)}	
No. of Outer players (Inner):	5 (5)	
No. of Mid-fielders (Neut):	7(0)	
No. of Att/Def Mid-fielders:	(4/3)	(3/4)

One-One-Two-One-One-Two-One-One

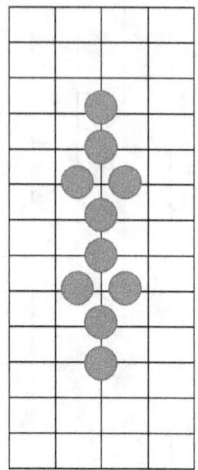

One-One-Two-One-One-Two-One-One

Playing Orientation: Neutral (5-5)

No. of Strikers /Def players: (1/1)

Shape: Hexagon

Shape spread: (3X8)

No. of half-side players (Neut): 8{(2(6)}

No. of Outer players (Inner): 6 (4)

No. of Mid-fielders (Neut): 8(0)

No. of Att/Def Mid-fielders: (4/4)

One-One-Three-One-One-One-One-One and One-One-One-One-One-Three-One-One

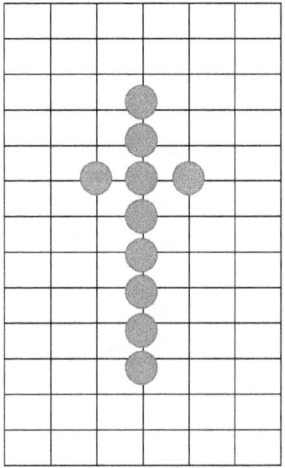

	One-One-Three-One-One-One-One-One	One-One-One-One-One-Three-One-One
Playing Orientation:	Attacking (4-6)	Defensive (6-4)
No. of Strikers /Def players:	(1/1)	(1/1)
Shape:	Quadrilateral	
Shape spread:	(3X8)	
No. of half-side players (Neut):	9{(1(8)}	
No. of Outer players (Inner):	4 (6)	
No. of Mid-fielders (Neut):	8(0)	
No. of Att/Def Mid-fielders:	(5/3)	(3/5)

One-Two-One-One-One-One-One-Two and Two-One-One-One-One-One-Two-One

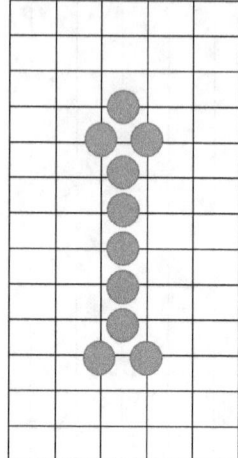

	One-Two-One-One-One-One-One-Two	Two-One-One-One-One-One-Two-One
Playing Orientation:	Neutral (5-5)	
No. of Strikers /Def players:	(1/2)	(2/1)
Shape:	Pentagon	
Shape spread:	(3X8)	
No. of half-side players (Neut):	8{(2(6)}	
No. of Outer players (Inner):	5 (5)	
No. of Mid-fielders (Neut):	7(0)	
No. of Att/Def Mid-fielders:	(4/3)	(3/4)

One-Two-One-One-One-One-Two-One

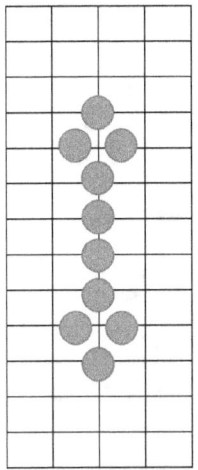

One-Two-One-One-One-One-Two-One

Playing Orientation: Neutral (5-5)
No. of Strikers /Def players: (1/1)
Shape: Hexagon
Shape spread: (3X8)
No. of half-side players (Neut): 8{(2(6)}
No. of Outer players (Inner): 6 (4)
No. of Mid-fielders (Neut): 8(0)
No. of Att/Def Mid-fielders: (4/4)

One-Two-One-One-One-Two-One-One and One-One-Two-One-One-One-Two-One

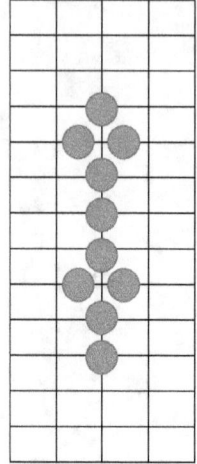

	One-Two-One-One-One-Two-One-One	One-One-Two-One-One-One-Two-One
Playing Orientation:	Neutral (5-5)	
No. of Strikers /Def players:	(1/1)	(1/1)
Shape:	Hexagon	
Shape spread:	(3X8)	
No. of half-side players (Neut):	8{(2(6)}	
No. of Outer players (Inner):	6 (4)	
No. of Mid-fielders (Neut):	8(0)	
No. of Att/Def Mid-fielders:	(4/4)	(4/4)

One-Two-One-One-Two-One-One-One and One-One-One-Two-One-One-Two-One

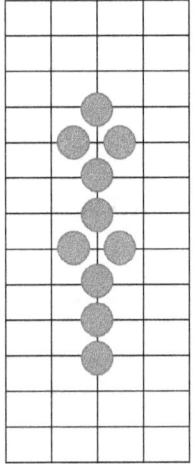

	One-Two-One-One-Two-One-One-One	One-One-One-Two-One-One-Two-One
Playing Orientation:	Neutral (5-5)	
No. of Strikers /Def players:	(1/1)	(1/1)
Shape:	Hexagon	
Shape spread:	(3X8)	
No. of half-side players (Neut):	8{(2(6)}	
No. of Outer players (Inner):	6 (4)	
No. of Mid-fielders (Neut):	8(0)	
No. of Att/Def Mid-fielders:	(4/4)	(4/4)

One-Two-One-Two-One-One-One-One and One-One-One-One-Two-One-Two-One

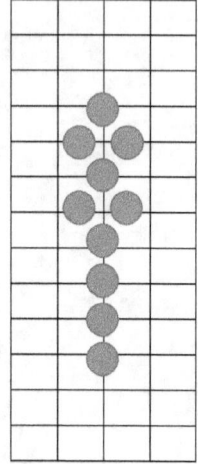

	One-Two-One-Two-One-One-One-One	One-One-One-One-Two-One-Two-One
Playing Orientation:	Attacking (4-6)	Defensive (6-4)
No. of Strikers /Def players:	(1/1)	(1/1)
Shape:	Hexagon	
Shape spread:	(3X8)	
No. of half-side players (Neut):	8{(2(6)}	
No. of Outer players (Inner):	6 (4)	
No. of Mid-fielders (Neut):	8(0)	
No. of Att/Def Mid-fielders:	(5/3)	(3/5)

One-Two-Two-One-One-One-One-One and One-One-One-One-One-Two-Two-One

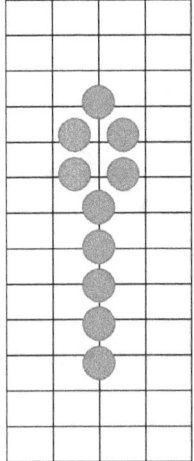

	One-Two-Two-One-One-One-One-One	One-One-One-One-One-Two-Two-One
Playing Orientation:	Attacking (4-6)	Defensive (6-4)
No. of Strikers /Def players:	(1/1)	(1/1)
Shape:	Hexagon	
Shape spread:	(3X8)	
No. of half-side players (Neut):	8{(2(6)}	
No. of Outer players (Inner):	6 (4)	
No. of Mid-fielders (Neut):	8(0)	
No. of Att/Def Mid-fielders:	(5/3)	(3/5)

One-Three-One-One-One-One-One-One and One-One-One-One-One-One-Three-One

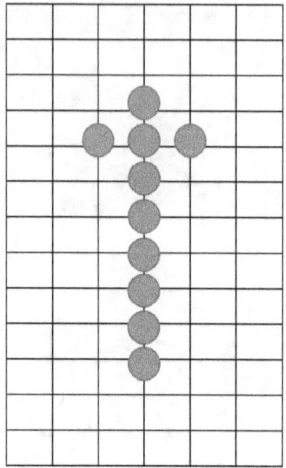

	One-Three-One-One-One-One-One-One	One-One-One-One-One-One-Three-One
Playing Orientation:	Attacking (4-6)	Defensive (6-4)
No. of Strikers /Def players:	(1/1)	(1/1)
Shape:	Quadrilateral	
Shape spread:	(3X8)	
No. of half-side players (Neut):	9{(1(8)}	
No. of Outer players (Inner):	4 (6)	
No. of Mid-fielders (Neut):	8(0)	
No. of Att/Def Mid-fielders:	(5/3)	(3/5)

Two-One-One-One-One-One-One-Two

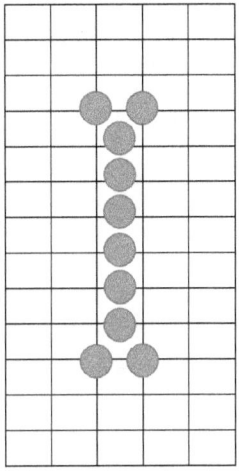

                           Two-One-One-One-One-One-One-Two

Playing Orientation:	Neutral (5-5)
No. of Strikers /Def players:	(2/2)
Shape:	Rectangle
Shape spread:	(3X8)
No. of half-side players (Neut):	8{(2(6)}
No. of Outer players (Inner):	4 (6)
No. of Mid-fielders (Neut):	6(0)
No. of Att/Def Mid-fielders:	(3/3)

LEVEL 9

Formations: 9

Symmetrically neutral: 1

One-One-One-One-One-One-One-One-Two and Two-One-One-One-One-One-One-One-One

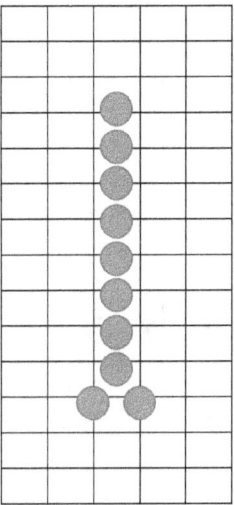

	One-One-One-One-One-One-One-One-Two	Two-One-One-One-One-One-One-One-One
Playing Orientation:	Defensive (6-5)	Attacking (5-6)
No. of Strikers /Def players:	(1/2)	(2/1)
Shape:	Triangle	
Shape spread:	(3X9)	
No. of half-side players (Neut):	9{(1(8)}	
No. of Outer players (Inner):	3 (7)	
No. of Mid-fielders (Neut):	7(1)	
No. of Att/Def Mid-fielders:	(3/3)	(3/3)

One-One-One-One-One-One-Two-One-One and One-One-Two-One-One-One-One-One-One

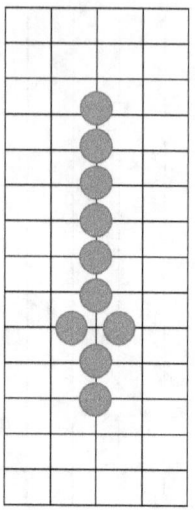

	One-One-One-One-One-One-Two-One-One	One-One-Two-One-One-One-One-One-One
Playing Orientation:	Defensive (6-5)	Attacking (5-6)
No. of Strikers /Def players:	(1/1)	(1/1)
Shape:	Quadrilateral	
Shape spread:	(3X9)	
No. of half-side players (Neut):	9{(1(8)}	
No. of Outer players (Inner):	4 (6)	
No. of Mid-fielders (Neut):	8(1)	
No. of Att/Def Mid-fielders:	(3/4)	(4/3)

One-One-One-One-One-Two-One-One-One and One-One-One-Two-One-One-One-One-One

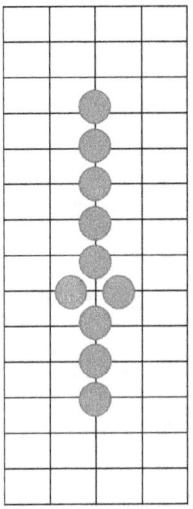

	One-One-One-One-One-Two-One-One-One	One-One-One-Two-One-One-One-One-One
Playing Orientation:	Defensive (6-5)	Attacking (5-6)
No. of Strikers /Def players:	(1/1)	(1/1)
Shape:	Quadrilateral	
Shape spread:	(3X9)	
No. of half-side players (Neut):	9{(1(8)}	
No. of Outer players (Inner):	4 (6)	
No. of Mid-fielders (Neut):	8(1)	
No. of Att/Def Mid-fielders:	(3/4)	(4/3)

One-One-One-One-Two-One-One-One-One

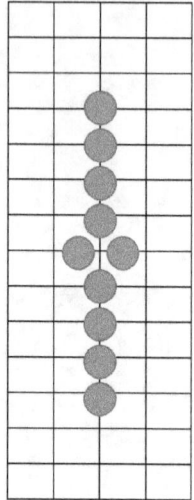

	One-One-One-One-Two-One-One-One-One
Playing Orientation:	Neutral (6-6)
No. of Strikers /Def players:	(1/1)
Shape:	Quadrilateral
Shape spread:	(3X9)
No. of half-side players (Neut):	9{(1(8)}
No. of Outer players (Inner):	4 (6)
No. of Mid-fielders (Neut):	8(2)
No. of Att/Def Mid-fielders:	(3/3)

One-Two-One-One-One-One-One-One-One and One-One-One-One-One-One-One-Two-One

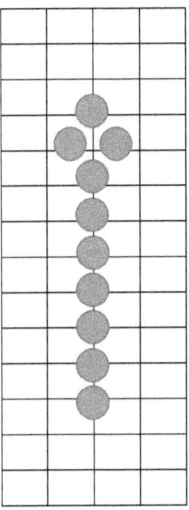

	One-Two-One-One-One-One-One-One-One	One-One-One-One-One-One-One-Two-One
Playing Orientation:	Attacking (5-6)	(6-5)
No. of Strikers /Def players:	(1/1)	(1/1)
Shape:	Quadrilateral	
Shape spread:	(3X9)	
No. of half-side players (Neut):	9{(1(8)}	
No. of Outer players (Inner):	4 (6)	
No. of Mid-fielders (Neut):	8(1)	
No. of Att/Def Mid-fielders:	(4/3)	(3/4)

LEVEL 10

Formations: 1

Symmetrically neutral: 1

One-One-One-One-One-One-One-One-One-One (B)

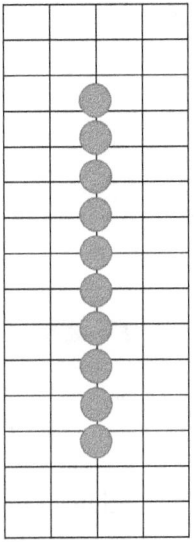

One-One-One-One-One-One-One-One-One-One (B)

Playing Orientation:	Neutral (5-5)
No. of Strikers /Def players:	(1/1)
Shape:	Linear
Shape spread:	(1X10)
No. of half-side players (Neut):	10{(0(10)}
No. of Outer players (Inner):	10 (0)
No. of Mid-fielders (Neut):	8(0)
No. of Att/Def Mid-fielders:	(4/4)

END

Formation Index

E

Eight-One-One, 18
Eight-Two, 13

F

Five-Five, 16
Five-Four-One, 21
Five-One-Four, 36
Five-One-One-One-One-One, 151
Five-One-One-One-Two, 130
Five-One-One-Three, 77
Five-One-One-Two-One, 104
Five-One-Three-One, 52
Five-One-Two-One-One, 90
Five-One-Two-Two, 69
Five-Three-One-One, 41
Five-Three-Two, 28
Five-Two-One-One-One, 85
Five-Two-One-Two, 65
Five-Two-Three, 33
Five-Two-Two-One, 47
Four-Five-One, 22
Four-Four-One-One, 42
Four-Four-Two, 29
Four-One-Five, 36
Four-One-Four-One, 57
Four-One-One-Four, 82
Four-One-One-One-One-One-One, 218
Four-One-One-One-One-Two, 202
Four-One-One-One-Three, 147
Four-One-One-One-Two-One, 175
Four-One-One-Three-One, 118
Four-One-One-Two-One-One, 162
Four-One-One-Two-Two, 138
Four-One-Three-One-One, 94
Four-One-Three-Two, 72
Four-One-Two-One-One-One, 155
Four-One-Two-One-Two, 133
Four-One-Two-Three, 80
Four-One-Two-Two-One, 109
Four-Six, 15
Four-Three-One-One-One, 86
Four-Three-One-Two, 66
Four-Three-Three, 34
Four-Three-Two-One, 48
Four-Two-Four, 37
Four-Two-One-One-One-One, 152
Four-Two-One-One-Two, 131
Four-Two-One-Three, 78
Four-Two-One-Two-One, 106
Four-Two-Three-One, 53
Four-Two-Two-One-One, 91
Four-Two-Two-Two, 70

N

Nine-One, 12

O

One-Eight-One, 25
One-Five-Four, 22
One-Five-One-One-One-One, 154
One-Five-One-One-Two, 129
One-Five-One-Three, 61
One-Five-One-Two-One, 105
One-Five-Three-One, 56
One-Five-Two-One-One, 93
One-Five-Two-Two, 62
One-Four-Five, 21
One-Four-Four-One, 60
One-Four-One-Four, 57
One-Four-One-One-One-One-One, 256
One-Four-One-One-One-Two, 199
One-Four-One-One-Three, 126
One-Four-One-One-Two-One, 178
One-Four-One-Three-One, 121
One-Four-One-Two-One-One, 200
One-Four-One-Two-Two, 127
One-Four-Three-One-One, 97
One-Four-Three-Two, 59

292

One-Four-Two-One-One-One, 201

One-Four-Two-One-Two, 128

One-Four-Two-Three, 58

One-Four-Two-Two-One, 112

One-Nine, 12

One-One-Eight, 18

One-One-Five-One-One-One, 161

One-One-Five-One-Two, 101

One-One-Five-Three, 43

One-One-Five-Two-One, 102

One-One-Four-Four, 42

One-One-Four-One-One-One-One, 238

One-One-Four-One-One-Two, 172

One-One-Four-One-Three, 98

One-One-Four-One-Two-One, 173

One-One-Four-Three-One, 100

One-One-Four-Two-One-One, 174

One-One-Four-Two-Two, 99

One-One-One-Five-One-One, 161

One-One-One-Five-Two, 88

One-One-One-Four-One-One-One, 228

One-One-One-Four-One-Two, 159

One-One-One-Four-Three, 87

One-One-One-Four-Two-One, 160

One-One-One-One-Five-One, 154

One-One-One-One-Four-One-One, 238

One-One-One-One-Four-Two, 215

One-One-One-One-One-Five, 151

One-One-One-One-One-Four-One, 256

One-One-One-One-One-One-Four, 218

One-One-One-One-One-One-One-One-One (A), 10

One-One-One-One-One-One-One-One-One (B), 290

One-One-One-One-One-One-One-Two, 284

One-One-One-One-One-One-Three, 263

One-One-One-One-One-Two-One, 288

One-One-One-One-One-Three-One, 281

One-One-One-One-One-Two-One-One, 285

One-One-One-One-One-Two-Two, 264

One-One-One-One-One-Three-One-One, 274

One-One-One-One-One-Three-Two, 261

One-One-One-One-Two-One-One-One, 286

One-One-One-One-Two-One-Two, 265

One-One-One-One-Two-Three, 219

One-One-One-One-One-Two-Two-One, 280

One-One-One-One-Six, 84

One-One-One-One-Three-One-One-One, 268

One-One-One-One-Three-One-Two, 222

One-One-One-One-Three-Three, 153

One-One-One-One-Three-Two-One, 251

One-One-One-One-Two-Four, 152

One-One-One-One-Two-One-One-One, 287

One-One-One-One-Two-One-One-Two, 266

One-One-One-One-Two-One-Three, 220

One-One-One-One-Two-One-Two-One, 279

One-One-One-One-Two-Three-One, 255

One-One-One-One-Two-Two-One-One, 267

One-One-One-One-Two-Two-Two, 221

One-One-One-Seven, 39

One-One-One-Six-One, 89

One-One-One-Three-Four, 86

One-One-One-Three-One-One-One-One, 268

One-One-One-Three-One-One-Two, 226

One-One-One-Three-One-Three, 157

One-One-One-Three-One-Two-One, 247

One-One-One-Three-Three-One, 198

One-One-One-Three-Two-One-One, 227

One-One-One-Three-Two-Two, 158

One-One-One-Two-Five, 85

One-One-One-Two-Four-One, 201

One-One-One-Two-One-Four, 155

One-One-One-Two-One-One-One-One, 286

One-One-One-Two-One-One-One-Two, 269

One-One-One-Two-One-One-Three, 223

One-One-One-Two-One-One-Two-One, 278

One-One-One-Two-One-Three-One, 254

One-One-One-Two-One-Two-One-One, 270

One-One-One-Two-One-Two-Two, 224

One-One-One-Two-Three-One-One, 237

One-One-One-Two-Three-Two, 214

One-One-One-Two-Two-One-One-One, 271

One-One-One-Two-Two-One-Two, 225

One-One-One-Two-Two-Three, 156

One-One-One-Two-Two-Two-One, 250

One-One-Seven-One, 45

One-One-Six-One-One, 103

One-One-Six-Two, 44

One-One-Three-Five, 41

One-One-Three-Four-One, 97

One-One-Three-One-Four, 94

One-One-Three-One-One-One-One-One, 274

One-One-Three-One-One-One-Two, 234

One-One-Three-One-One-Three, 167

One-One-Three-One-One-Two-One, 235

One-One-Three-One-Three-One, 169

One-One-Three-One-Two-One-One, 236

One-One-Three-One-Two-Two, 168

One-One-Three-Three-One-One, 171

One-One-Three-Three-Two, 96

One-One-Three-Two-One-One-One, 237

One-One-Three-Two-One-Two, 170

One-One-Three-Two-Three, 95

One-One-Three-Two-Two-One, 189

One-One-Two-Five-One, 93

One-One-Two-Four-One-One, 174

One-One-Two-Four-Two, 146

One-One-Two-One-Five, 90

One-One-Two-One-Four-One, 200

One-One-Two-One-One-Four, 162

One-One-Two-One-One-One-One-One-One, 285

One-One-Two-One-One-One-One-One-Two, 272

One-One-Two-One-One-One-One-Three, 229

One-One-Two-One-One-One-Two-One, 277

One-One-Two-One-One-Three-One, 253

One-One-Two-One-One-Two-One-One, 273

One-One-Two-One-One-Two-Two, 230

One-One-Two-One-Three-One-One, 236

One-One-Two-One-Three-Two, 213

One-One-Two-One-Two-One-One-One, 270

One-One-Two-One-Two-One-Two, 231

One-One-Two-One-Two-Three, 163

One-One-Two-One-Two-Two-One, 249

One-One-Two-Six, 40

One-One-Two-Three-One-One-One, 227

One-One-Two-Three-One-Two, 166

One-One-Two-Three-Three, 92

One-One-Two-Three-Two-One, 191

One-One-Two-Two-Four, 91

294

One-One-Two-Two-One-One-One-One, 267

One-One-Two-Two-One-One-Two, 232

One-One-Two-Two-One-Three, 164

One-One-Two-Two-One-Two-One, 246

One-One-Two-Two-Three-One, 197

One-One-Two-Two-Two-One-One, 233

One-One-Two-Two-Two-Two, 165

One-Seven-One-One, 45

One-Seven-Two, 24

One-Six-One-One-One, 89

One-Six-One-Two, 63

One-Six-Three, 23

One-Six-Two-One, 51

One-Three-Five-One, 56

One-Three-Four-One-One, 100

One-Three-Four-Two, 55

One-Three-One-Five, 52

One-Three-One-Four-One, 121

One-Three-One-One-Four, 118

One-Three-One-One-One-One-One, 281

One-Three-One-One-One-Two, 252

One-Three-One-One-One-Three, 192

One-Three-One-One-One-Two-One, 241

One-Three-One-One-Three-One, 194

One-Three-One-One-Two-One-One, 253

One-Three-One-One-Two-Two, 193

One-Three-One-Three-One-One, 169

One-Three-One-Three-Two, 120

One-Three-One-Two-One-One-One, 254

One-Three-One-Two-One-Two, 195

One-Three-One-Two-Three, 119

One-Three-One-Two-Two-One, 186

One-Three-Six, 20

One-Three-Three-One-One-One, 198

One-Three-Three-One-Two, 125

One-Three-Three-Three, 54

One-Three-Three-Two-One, 115

One-Three-Two-Four, 53

One-Three-Two-One-One-One, 255

One-Three-Two-One-One-Two, 196

One-Three-Two-One-Three, 122

One-Three-Two-One-Two-One, 181

One-Three-Two-Three-One, 123

One-Three-Two-Two-One-One, 197

One-Three-Two-Two-Two, 124

One-Two-Five-One-One, 102

One-Two-Five-Two, 50

One-Two-Four-One-One-One, 160

One-Two-Four-One-Two, 116

One-Two-Four-Three, 49

One-Two-Four-Two-One, 117

One-Two-One-Five-One, 105

One-Two-One-Four-One-One, 173

One-Two-One-Four-Two, 108

One-Two-One-One-Five, 104

One-Two-One-One-Four-One, 178

One-Two-One-One-One-Four, 175

One-Two-One-One-One-One-One-One, 288

One-Two-One-One-One-One-One-Two, 275

One-Two-One-One-One-One-Three, 239

One-Two-One-One-One-One-Two-One, 276

One-Two-One-One-One-Three-One, 241

One-Two-One-One-One-Two-One-One, 277

One-Two-One-One-One-Two-Two, 240

One-Two-One-One-Three-One-One, 235

One-Two-One-One-Three-Two, 177

One-Two-One-One-Two-One-One-One, 278

295

One-Two-One-One-Two-One-Two, 242

One-Two-One-One-Two-Three, 176

One-Two-One-One-Two-Two-One, 243

One-Two-One-Six, 46

One-Two-One-Three-One-One-One, 247

One-Two-One-Three-One-Two, 182

One-Two-One-Three-Three, 107

One-Two-One-Three-Two-One, 183

One-Two-One-Two-Four, 106

One-Two-One-Two-One-One-One-One, 279

One-Two-One-Two-One-One-Two, 244

One-Two-One-Two-One-Three, 179

One-Two-One-Two-One-Two-One, 245

One-Two-One-Two-Three-One, 181

One-Two-One-Two-Two-One-One, 246

One-Two-One-Two-Two-Two, 180

One-Two-Seven, 19

One-Two-Six-One, 51

One-Two-Three-Four, 48

One-Two-Three-One-One-One-One, 251

One-Two-Three-One-One-Two, 190

One-Two-Three-One-Three, 113

One-Two-Three-One-Two-One, 183

One-Two-Three-Three-One, 115

One-Two-Three-Two-One-One, 191

One-Two-Three-Two-Two, 114

One-Two-Two-Five, 47

One-Two-Two-Four-One, 112

One-Two-Two-One-Four, 109

One-Two-Two-One-One-One-One, 280

One-Two-Two-One-One-One-Two, 248

One-Two-Two-One-One-Three, 184

One-Two-Two-One-One-Two-One, 243

One-Two-Two-One-Three-One, 186

One-Two-Two-One-Two-One-One, 249

One-Two-Two-One-Two-Two, 185

One-Two-Two-Three-One-One, 189

One-Two-Two-Three-Two, 111

One-Two-Two-Two-One-One-One, 250

One-Two-Two-Two-One-Two, 187

One-Two-Two-Two-Three, 110

One-Two-Two-Two-Two-One, 188

S

Seven-One-One-One, 39

Seven-One-Two, 26

Seven-Three, 14

Seven-Two-One, 19

Six-Four, 15

Six-One-One-One-One, 84

Six-One-One-Two, 64

Six-One-Three, 32

Six-One-Two-One, 46

Six-Three-One, 20

Six-Two-One-One, 40

Six-Two-Two, 27

T

Three-Five-One-One, 43

Three-Five-Two, 30

Three-Four-One-One-One, 87

Three-Four-One-Two, 67

Three-Four-Three, 35

Three-Four-Two-One, 49

Three-One-Five-One, 61

Three-One-Four-One-One, 98

Three-One-Four-Two, 75

Three-One-One-Five, 77

Three-One-One-Four-One, 126

Three-One-One-One-Four, 147

Three-One-One-One-One-One-One, 263

Three-One-One-One-One-One-Two, 257

Three-One-One-One-One-Three, 216

Three-One-One-One-One-Two-One, 239

Three-One-One-One-Three-One, 192

Three-One-One-One-Two-One-One, 229

Three-One-One-One-Two-Two, 210

Three-One-One-Three-One-One, 167

Three-One-One-Three-Two, 142

Three-One-One-Two-One-One-One, 223

Three-One-One-Two-One-Two, 207

Three-One-One-Two-Three, 148

Three-One-One-Two-Two-One, 184

Three-One-Six, 32

Three-One-Three-One-One-One, 157

Three-One-Three-One-Two, 135

Three-One-Three-Three, 79

Three-One-Three-Two-One, 113

Three-One-Two-Four, 78

Three-One-Two-One-One-One-One, 220

Three-One-Two-One-One-Two, 204

Three-One-Two-One-Three, 149

Three-One-Two-One-Two-One, 179

Three-One-Two-Three-One, 122

Three-One-Two-Two-One-One, 164

Three-One-Two-Two-Two, 140

Three-Seven, 14

Three-Six-One, 23

Three-Three-Four, 34

Three-Three-One-One-One-One, 153

Three-Three-One-One-Two, 132

Three-Three-One-Three, 79

Three-Three-One-Two-One, 107

Three-Three-Three-One, 54

Three-Three-Two-One-One, 92

Three-Three-Two-Two, 71

Three-Two-Five, 33

Three-Two-Four-One, 58

Three-Two-One-Four, 80

Three-Two-One-One-One-One, 219

Three-Two-One-One-One-Two, 203

Three-Two-One-One-Three, 148

Three-Two-One-One-Two-One, 176

Three-Two-One-Three-One, 119

Three-Two-One-Two-One-One, 163

Three-Two-One-Two-Two, 139

Three-Two-Three-One-One, 95

Three-Two-Three-Two, 73

Three-Two-Two-One-One-One, 156

Three-Two-Two-One-Two, 134

Three-Two-Two-Three, 81

Three-Two-Two-Two-One, 110

Two-Eight, 13

Two-Five-One-One-One, 88

Two-Five-One-Two, 68

Two-Five-Three, 30

Two-Five-Two-One, 50

Two-Four-Four, 29

Two-Four-One-One-One-One, 215

Two-Four-One-One-Two, 145

Two-Four-One-Three, 75

Two-Four-One-Two-One, 108

Two-Four-Three-One, 55

Two-Four-Two-One-One, 146

Two-Four-Two-Two, 76

Two-One-Five-One-One, 101

Two-One-Five-Two, 68

Two-One-Four-One-One-One, 159

Two-One-Four-One-Two, 137

Two-One-Four-Three, 67

Two-One-Four-Two-One, 116

Two-One-One-Five-One, 129

Two-One-One-Four-One-One, 172

Two-One-One-Four-Two, 145

Two-One-One-One-Five, 130

Two-One-One-One-Four-One, 199
Two-One-One-One-One-Four, 202
Two-One-One-One-One-One-One-One-One, 284
Two-One-One-One-One-One-One-Two, 282
Two-One-One-One-One-One-Three, 257
Two-One-One-One-One-One-Two-One, 275
Two-One-One-One-One-Three-One, 252
Two-One-One-One-One-Two-One-One, 272
Two-One-One-One-One-Two-Two, 258
Two-One-One-One-Three-One-One, 234
Two-One-One-One-Three-Two, 212
Two-One-One-One-Two-One-One-One, 269
Two-One-One-One-Two-One-Two, 259
Two-One-One-One-Two-Three, 203
Two-One-One-One-Two-Two-One, 248
Two-One-One-Six, 64
Two-One-One-Three-One-One-One, 226
Two-One-One-Three-One-Two, 206
Two-One-One-Three-Three, 132
Two-One-One-Three-Two-One, 190

Two-One-One-Two-Four, 131
Two-One-One-Two-One-One-One-One, 266
Two-One-One-Two-One-One-Two, 260
Two-One-One-Two-One-Three, 204
Two-One-One-Two-One-Two-One, 244
Two-One-One-Two-Three-One, 196
Two-One-One-Two-Two-One-One, 232
Two-One-One-Two-Two-Two, 205
Two-One-Seven, 26
Two-One-Six-One, 63
Two-One-Three-Four, 66
Two-One-Three-One-One-One-One, 222
Two-One-Three-One-One-Two, 206
Two-One-Three-One-Three, 135
Two-One-Three-One-Two-One, 182
Two-One-Three-Three-One, 125
Two-One-Three-Two-One-One, 166
Two-One-Three-Two-Two, 136
Two-One-Two-Five, 65
Two-One-Two-Four-One, 128
Two-One-Two-One-Four, 133
Two-One-Two-One-One-One-One-One, 265

Two-One-Two-One-One-One-Two, 259
Two-One-Two-One-One-Three, 207
Two-One-Two-One-One-Two-One, 242
Two-One-Two-One-Three-One, 195
Two-One-Two-One-Two-One-One, 231
Two-One-Two-One-Two-Two, 208
Two-One-Two-Three-One-One, 170
Two-One-Two-Three-Two, 144
Two-One-Two-Two-One-One-One, 225
Two-One-Two-Two-One-Two, 209
Two-One-Two-Two-Three, 134
Two-One-Two-Two-Two-One, 187
Two-Seven-One, 24
Two-Six-One-One, 44
Two-Six-Two, 31
Two-Three-Five, 28
Two-Three-Four-One, 59
Two-Three-One-Four, 72
Two-Three-One-One-One-One, 261
Two-Three-One-One-One-Two, 212
Two-Three-One-One-Three, 142
Two-Three-One-One-Two-One, 177

Two-Three-One-Three-One, 120

Two-Three-One-Two-One-One, 213

Two-Three-One-Two-Two, 143

Two-Three-Three-One-One, 96

Two-Three-Three-Two, 74

Two-Three-Two-One-One-One, 214

Two-Three-Two-One-Two, 144

Two-Three-Two-Three, 73

Two-Three-Two-Two-One, 111

Two-Two-Five-One, 62

Two-Two-Four-One-One, 99

Two-Two-Four-Two, 76

Two-Two-One-Five, 69

Two-Two-One-Four-One, 127

Two-Two-One-One-Four, 138

Two-Two-One-One-One-One-One-One, 264

Two-Two-One-One-One-One-Two, 258

Two-Two-One-One-One-Three, 210

Two-Two-One-One-One-Two-One, 240

Two-Two-One-One-Three-One, 193

Two-Two-One-One-Two-One-One, 230

Two-Two-One-One-Two-Two, 211

Two-Two-One-Three-One-One, 168

Two-Two-One-Three-Two, 143

Two-Two-One-Two-One-One-One, 224

Two-Two-One-Two-One-Two, 208

Two-Two-One-Two-Three, 139

Two-Two-One-Two-Two-One, 185

Two-Two-Six, 27

Two-Two-Three-One-One-One, 158

Two-Two-Three-One-Two, 136

Two-Two-Three-Three, 71

Two-Two-Three-Two-One, 114

Two-Two-Two-Four, 70

Two-Two-Two-One-One-One-One, 221

Two-Two-Two-One-One-Two, 205

Two-Two-Two-One-Three, 140

Two-Two-Two-One-Two-One, 180

Two-Two-Two-Three-One, 124

Two-Two-Two-Two-One-One, 165

Two-Two-Two-Two-Two, 141

www.ingramcontent.com/pod-product-compliance
Lightning Source LLC
Chambersburg PA
CBHW071806300426
44116CB00009B/1222